TRUTH, BEAUTY AND GOODNESS

Steiner-Waldorf Education as a
Demand of Our Time

D1457836

Books by the same Author:

Steiner Education in Theory and Practice
Education and Beyond
Rudolf Steiner: His Life and Work
The Realities of Prayer
Understand YOUR Temperament!
Your Reincarnating Child (with Sylvia Childs)
From Birthlessness to Deathlessness
5 + 7 = 12 Senses
An Imp on Either Shoulder
The Journey Continues ... (with Sylvia Childs)
Balancing Your Temperament

TRUTH, BEAUTY AND GOODNESS

Steiner-Waldorf Education as a Demand of Our Time

An Esoteric Study

Dr Gilbert Childs

TEMPLE LODGE
London

Temple Lodge Publishing
51 Queen Caroline Street
London W6 9QL

Published by Temple Lodge 1999

A catalogue record for this book is available from the British Library

ISBN 1 902636 05 8

Cover by Studio MAOSS
Typeset by DP Photosetting, Aylesbury, Bucks
Printed and bound in Great Britain by Cromwell Press Limited, Trowbridge, Wiltshire

Contents

In thy Thinking World-wide Thoughts are living,
In thy Feeling World-All Forces weaving,
In thy Willing World-Beings working.
Lose thyself in World-extensive Thoughts,
Feel thyself through World-All Forces,
Create thyself from Beings of Will.
Linger not in faraway Worlds
In dreamy play of thought;
Begin in the vast reaches of the Spirit,
And end in thine own Being's depths,
Where thou shalt find eternal aims of Gods
Knowing thyself in thee.

Rudolf Steiner

Introduction

Rudolf Steiner argued that subjects comprising any school curriculum should be regarded not so much as a body of knowledge to be transmitted by teachers and learned by pupils, but rather that the various subjects should be orchestrated by teachers for the purpose of exercising pupils' soul-faculties of Thinking, Feeling and Willing. These basic human faculties manifest in civilization as the 'Eternal Verities' of Truth, Beauty and Goodness, and these in turn in the three main areas of human endeavour, namely, Science, Art and Religion, all respectively.

The sources and nature of these nine (3 × 3) factors in the evolutionary phases of the Earth and mankind are identified and reviewed, as are the many correlations, parallels and other connections within and between the elegant models and patterns which emerge. Determinants such as polarities and their equilibrium, metamorphosis and transmutation, recurrence and recapitulation, reversal and reciprocity are all indicated, and their functions discussed.

The aim of this book is twofold: to substantiate the assertion by Rudolf Steiner that his philosophy and practice of education arose as a demand of the age in which we are living, and to gather together correlated material in order to illustrate the practical application of the nine factors mentioned. I have therefore outlined the essential evolutionary archetypes and their main functions as acknowledged by spiritual science. These factors, and many other threefold patterns, are discussed at considerable depth in evolutionary and historical terms. The very orderliness of Creation makes it possible for the unmanifest as well as the manifest elements involved to be examined and appraised, and glimpses into the evolution and progression of the whole human race, the conditions and circumstances our ancestors underwent and what our descendants are likely to experience, appear throughout the text. I have also been careful to include, when appropriate to do so, reminders of our spiritual origins and our meticulously ordered soul-spiritual and bodily constitution, as well as indicating supportive evidence.

The sheer grandeur and elegance that emerges by reason of such patterns and configurations is not readily apparent when regarded as mere abstractions; for them to be more fully understood they have to be regarded as the concrete realities they are. The archetypal agencies involved are recognized as being sweepingly comprehensive, irresistibly powerful and comfortingly consistent in their workings. Evidence of the powerful agencies at work in the overall evolution of the Earth and of the development and education of the human race it supports reveals a truly grand and inspiring panorama, in which Steiner's educational philosophy and practice can not only be recognized as valid but also that its operations are indeed in genuine harmony with the demands of the present age as well as those of the immediate future.

Agents, Agencies and Archetypes

Remember that there are beings in the spiritual world who correspond to the abstract ideals of Truth, Beauty and Goodness that we encounter on Earth. It is towards these beings of the higher hierarchies—not merely towards abstract ideals—that the human soul is once more moving as we pursue our ideals and activities.[1]

Truth, Beauty and Goodness as archetypal agencies

The lofty ideals of Truth, Beauty and Goodness underpin civilization itself, and are by tradition referred to as the 'Eternal Verities'; but although by convention they are three in number there is, as we shall see in due course, a fourth Verity, namely Justice. Whereas the principle of threefolding is seen to dominate the numerous patterns that reveal themselves, that of fourfolding is also of equal significance. All four Verities are true prototypes in nature and character, and by reference to the chapter quotation above it can be concluded that exalted spiritual beings are involved in their realization in Earthly, and by inference human, affairs of every kind. Medieval thinkers considered, feasibly enough, that the prime Verity was Truth. They asserted that God or Christ represented the prime Verity, and was thus practically synonymous with Truth, which endures infinitely and for ever in past and future time. Nonetheless, Justice may with good reason be deemed to rival this primacy, as will be explained later on.

Into the universal scheme of things the notion of *archetype* fits very neatly, the ordinary dictionary definition describing it as the essential nature or idea of a thing as distinguished from the matter in which it is embodied, or an original model or type after which other similar things are patterned. Such an abstract explication corresponds to Plato's idea of 'forms' which, whilst existing in the unseen worlds, represent the 'idea' of every single manifestation of individual entities which are entirely standard. Common usage of the term often assumes the notions of Swiss psychologist Carl Gustav Jung (1875–1961), who regarded an archetype as an inherited idea or way of thinking derived from the 'collective unconscious' which he considered to represent the combined experience of humankind as a whole. Regardless of such notions, however, the term as employed throughout this book is in accord with anthroposophical spiritual science. Rudolf Steiner insisted that archetypes are not abstract ideas, but realities which actually exist in the spiritual worlds, and his explanation of them is characteristically graphic:

> [In the spiritual worlds are to be found] the spiritual archetypes of all things and beings which are present in the physical and soul worlds. Imagine the picture of a painter existing in his mind before it is painted. This gives an analogy to what is meant by the expression *archetype*. It does not concern us here that the painter has perhaps not had such an archetype in his mind before he paints, and that it only gradually develops and becomes complete during the execution of the picture. In the real world of spirit there exist such archetypes for all things, and the physical things and beings are copies of these archetypes.[2]

Granted that we accept this contention, the question is bound to arise: what is the origin of the archetype of three-folding? For the answer, however provisional to start with, we must look to our own constitution as human beings, and to the whole world of nature and the universe of which we are undeniably part. (The underlying principles of threefolding are discussed in the Appendix to this book.) Meanwhile, it is made abundantly clear in the intervening chapters that the principle of threefolding is firmly rooted in human civilization and culture, as there are so many phenomena perceivable in ourselves and society that accord with it which cannot possibly escape notice.

During the present Earth evolution we are able, indeed obliged, by very reason of our faculties of Thinking, Feeling and Willing, to express ourselves in society and the world by means of these agencies. Evidence of this is afforded by the threefold nature and structure of human endeavour in the fields of Science, Art and Religion respectively. In all this it should be borne in mind that these three fields of human endeavour existed *as a unity* in the Mystery Schools, and it was not until the Age of the Intellectual Soul dawned during the eighth century BC that the partitive process involving this particular trinity commenced.

Similarly, the very principles by which our civilization is sustained and progresses, namely, the noble ideals of Liberty, Equality and Fraternity, also exhibit the pattern of three-folding, and these, too, are related to the Eternal Verities. A further patterning of society which is evident in our daily lives concerns its economic, political and cultural aspects. Needless to say, there are definite interconnections among all these factors, some more obvious than others, and these are discussed in later chapters, where relationships with Rudolf Steiner's ideas with regard to the Threefold Social Order are examined.

Undoubtedly, the principle of threefolding exists as a law, and is the archetype of all archetypes where change is involved. The Godhead or Trinity is of a three-in-one and one-in-three constitution, and in this sense we are 'made in the image of God'. That we ourselves are organized in ways that are threefold in terms of body, soul and spirit is, to sound thinking, evident enough. The archetypes of Thinking, Feeling and Willing, which come to expression in ourselves and our communities as Truth, Beauty and Goodness respectively, are derived directly from the Beings of the First Hierarchy, namely, the Seraphim, Cherubim and Thrones. The four Verities of Justice, Truth, Beauty and Goodness function by virtue of their being incorporated as archetypal agencies into our constitution during the Old Saturn, Old Sun and Old Moon evolutions immediately prior to our present

Earthly manifestation, and currently, as will be described in later chapters.

The importance of balance

An important archetypal principle, if not an archetype itself, is that of *balance,* the maintenance of equilibrium. If one pan of the scale is up, the other must be down, and the desired state of stability is often very difficult to achieve. In this, we can discern the parallel model of antipathy and sympathy, and the constant swinging between the two. Furthermore, we know that nothing remains entirely static: either a situation, circumstance or condition is progressing or it is retrogressing, ameliorating or deteriorating, getting better or getting worse. So here we have the model of plus, minus and equals—that is to say, balance. But we also know that balancing acts are usually if not always precariously difficult to maintain, particularly so where human nature is involved.

There are obvious connotations in all this with the dialectic methodologies popularized by Hegel, which in general terms involve procedures which systematically weigh the merits of conflicting facts or ideas with a view to the resolution of their real or apparent contradictions. His method of raising an antithesis to oppose a given thesis, and thence by argument, analysis or further investigation arriving at a more or less satisfactory synthesis—which may then be utilized as a basis for a new thesis—is clearly threefold in its construction, and moreover reliable as a mode of operation.

In all this we are reminded of the two enormously powerful influences we human beings are inexorably subjected to—those of Lucifer and Ahriman. We cannot escape from these, as they are built into our very constitution. Our only hope is to balance out these influences.[3] Furthermore, we are very often able to detect two subsidiary and related qualities connected with this central, pivotal or balancing component which exists in the field of interaction between it and the two outer opposing factors. For example, the human soul is placed as it were midway between spirit and body, and is therefore able to influence both these members. Similarly, in the case of the human soul itself, *feeling* operates as an equilibrating force which affects the two associated faculties to which it is central, namely, *thinking* (antipathetic) and *willing* (sympathetic).

Now as it is these same faculties of the human soul, namely, Thinking, Feeling and Willing, which are expressed in every area of human concern already mentioned, notably as Science, Art and Religion, Truth, Beauty and Goodness, and Liberty, Equality and Fraternity respectively, the central concept of each one is invariably seen to function as a balancing factor. Indeed, certain Ahrimanic and Luciferic influences can be legitimately associated with these three important trichotomies, and they are constantly in need of being balanced out and maintained in reasonable proportion to one another.

We should neither hate nor fear either Lucifer or Ahriman; rather should we call in one in order to create a polarity to the other. We should ourselves strive to occupy the neutral central position, and thus become well placed to exploit the influences of both to our own advantage. This, surely, is how humanity should educate itself—by grasping Luciferic or Ahrimanic opportunities as they arise and by maximizing whatever benefits may accrue. Thus we have a valid model for the advancement of civilization. By balancing out the conservative, 'institutionary' influences of Ahriman against the revolutionary influences of Lucifer, we find *ourselves* in the pivotal position most likely to enhance the advancement of social welfare in particular, civilization in general, and even evolution itself.

Materialists are missing out

An enthusiastic upholder of the principle of threefolding was Francis Bacon of Verulam, (1561–1626). In his *Advancement and Proficience of Learning,* he constructed a Pyramid of

Philosophy from a whole system of trichotomies based on Divine Philosophy, Human Philosophy and Natural Philosophy. He and his collaborators were important harbingers of the Age of the Consciousness Soul, although it is clear from his writings that his original intentions included involvement on the soul and spiritual levels as well as that of matter.

His ideal and purpose was to implement what he called 'The Great Instauration', thus to lay the foundations of a movement which would bring about universal enlightenment, brotherhood and peace. Its premises and propositions related to the human spirit, soul and body respectively, but however valid and feasible his ideas were, they eventually dwindled down to materialism. The first aphorism of his *Novum Organon* reduces the human being to a mere observer and interpreter of nature—precisely descriptive of today's orthodox scientist: 'Man, as the minister and Interpreter of Nature, does and understands as much as his observation on the Order of Nature, either with regard to things or the mind, permits him, and neither knows nor is capable of more.' These words may be regarded as the final closing of the doors to the spiritual worlds of the ancients, and the opening of those to the new creed of materialism. The civilized world itself was about to be changed. Synonymous with change is metamorphosis, and all that is evolved, transformed and transmuted. Obviously, the object of a change may be the subject of the change, or vice versa. When we ourselves are changed in some way, we may and often will be the agent that brings the change about rather than some other factor.

For instance, both spiritual science and orthodox science recognize that every effect must have a prior cause. Yet when the latter ponders the 'beginnings of life' it actually poses *chance*, in the shape of a hypothesis which posits spontaneous emergence of life forms, or an original life form, from the primeval ooze, which itself must have had a prior cause also. The origins and evolution of the cosmos as delineated by Rudolf Steiner differs enormously from that posited by orthodox geologists. He goes into great detail concerning the activities of the various powerful spiritual beings and agencies which have been involved—and indeed still are—in the evolution of the Earth and ourselves as essentially and primarily spiritual beings.

As modern science is thoroughly materialistic in outlook and character, it cannot accept that God as Creator is the originator of life because it does not recognize spirit as a creative agent. Instead, it recognizes the Big Bang or some other physical factor as a kind of 'kick-start' agency, but this without determining—or even suggesting—a cause for it. In other words, it teaches that what is living arose from that which was lifeless and inert, and not the other way round.

However, the geologist Walther Cloos, in his book *The Living Earth,* demonstrates that everything that is inert and lifeless in terms of the mineral world has been *previously alive,* or derived from that which had once been living, as in the case of some metamorphic rocks. This suggests that the originator of this life, as change agent, is dynamic and *creative,* whereas the result or effect, namely, inert matter, is static and *created.* Hence science, at least hypothetically, is not able to accuse God of creating the universe *ex nihilo;* if so, the Big Bang likewise must have been created 'out of nothing'.

Rudolf Steiner maintained that where spiritual-scientific knowledge of the human being is concerned, there is no difference between theory and practice. Orthodox philosophy can do little more than introduce the notion of *parallelism,* which posits that to every mental change corresponds a concomitant, but causally unconnected, bodily alteration. This notion, and the 'other minds' hypothesis whereby, for example, we infer from the sight of a weeping person that he or she is sad because we ourselves weep when we are sad, he dismissed as invalid. We are not normally conscious of this kind of synchronous 'unity of action' involved because our very constitution does not ordinarily allow of it.

However, we must be capable of discerning the apparent

and not so apparent differences as well as the more obvious similarities, which arise in the field of tension linking any two polarities. In a certain sense, therefore, the similarities and differences form of themselves a unity. Hence, we can legitimately posit theory, practice, and how they are merged as conforming to our archetypal model of threefolding. At all times and in all circumstances spirit is anterior to matter, and in matter spirit is perpetually at work; thus the manner of this activity and its results equates to the operational field referred to.

The prime mover, the initiator, the actual *power* is essentially spiritual in nature, and is the dynamic agent, itself unmanifest, to which everything that is manifest is patient. In other words, all Creation is, in the final analysis, the result of the activities of spiritual forces. Spirit is indestructible, and therefore continuously ongoing in its ceaseless activities, whether normally manifest or unmanifest. All beings, from the highest hierarchy downwards, are necessarily in a state of endless metamorphosis, and are therefore constantly evolving.

In matters of perception and understanding, it would seem at first sight that the spiritual investigator and the scientific researcher are in polar opposition. Materialistic science necessarily rests squarely on the premise that the boundaries to the acquisition of knowledge coincide precisely with what is perceptible by the human senses and their extension by means of investigative instruments. Yet it can be demonstrated convincingly that our very constitution as physiological-psychological beings predisposes us to the establishment of such boundaries to our perception.[4] Such boundaries of knowledge do not actually exist, but have been placed there by philosophers and others who are not able sufficiently to discern and appreciate this aspect of our nature and constitution. There are no actual limits to knowledge—only self-delineated barriers.

Rudolf Steiner indicated how it is possible for all of us to cross the boundary between the sensible, material 'knowable' and the supersensible, immaterial 'unknowable'. Physical-material objects can be perceived only by means of bodily sense-organs. By the same token, supersensible phenomena are perceptible only by supersensible or spiritual organs; and these, maintained Steiner, are possessed—in an undeveloped state for the most part—by every human being. This capability, he declared, is available to every human being who is prepared to undergo the necessary training for it. In other words, just as it is perfectly possible within everyday experience to perceive, investigate and understand the material world around us, it is equally possible for us to learn to perceive and understand the immaterial, supersensible world; both worlds are entirely capable of being *known*. It is on grounds such as these that a genuine science of the spirit can be established and developed, and this is precisely what Steiner accomplished.

These issues are clearly of a philosophical nature, and Rudolf Steiner recognized the problems involved and sought to demonstrate their solution by philosophical argument. Trained as a scientist, he fully appreciated the empirical approach and methods associated with the disciplines of science. He was fully conscious of the fact that he would have to apply the same stringent and precise standards to his own mode of research into the supersensible, spiritual world as materialist scientists apply to theirs in the physical-material world. These he found to be equally reliable, to the extent of his declaring his life's aim to be the founding of new methods of spiritual research on a scientific basis.

He consistently showed that spiritual truths, and knowledge supersensibly acquired, are in complete and necessary agreement with the knowledge that can be gained from the world of the senses, that is to say, by scientific methodologies applicable to both worlds. Indeed, things cannot be otherwise; if to the 'half-reality' of sense-perception is added the complementary 'half-reality' of supersensible perception, the result can only be the whole, complete apprehension of total reality.

Material science has contributed enormously to the discovery and establishment of the so-called Laws of Nature. Its overriding value lies in the fact that it has discerned *order* in the whole *kosmos*, which Greek word can mean not only 'world' or 'universe'—and this directly on account of its 'perfect arrangement'—but also 'order' as antithetic to 'chaos'. Rudolf Steiner maintained that *order* is a principal characteristic of the spiritual world, and this should come as no surprise. The law of cause and effect is deemed crucial for a proper understanding of the material world, and as spirit is primary and creative, and matter secondary and created, it should be seen to apply also to the dynamic but unseen and directly undiscernible spiritual world. This is indeed the case; but whereas spiritual laws are entirely moral in character, those appertaining to the physical-material world are essentially mechanistic. Consequently, he was able to confirm that 'the moral world order is just as much predetermined in the spirit as causality is predetermined here on Earth.'[5]

The law of causality is operational in the supersensible realms also, but even though it is not always readily demonstrable by recourse to empirical methodologies, it does not signify that it is not applicable there. Moreover, since the laws and ordinances of the creative spiritual powers are utterly moral, it follows that natural laws must likewise show consistency and regularity, and lack any tendency to 'lie', or be deviant in any significant way. This 'perfect arrangement' of the orderings of Heaven as well as Earth is reflected in the ancient maxim 'As above, so below; as below, so above', which is widely acclaimed for the truth that it is. That which is material and spiritual, manifest and unmanifest must, in terms of the Whole, encompassing both material and spiritual worlds, sensory and supersensory, be co-existent, parallel and complementary. To bring about a fuller understanding of this truth must be our immediate and ongoing task.

Driving Forces in World Evolution

The Stars once spoke to Man.
It is World-destiny
That they are silent now.
To be aware of the silence
Can be grief to Earthly Man.

But in the deepening silence,
There grows and ripens
What Man speaks to the Stars.
To be aware of this speaking
Can become strength for Spirit-Man.[1]

A rough guide to the evolution of Earth and humanity

The 'Grand Plan' of the evolution of the planet Earth and its denizens posited by spiritual science is one of breathtaking proportions, and strikingly elegant in the patterns and designs that make them up in such orderly fashion. In this regard Rudolf Steiner confirmed many established tenets and traditional teachings from his own investigations into the supersensible worlds. He never accepted them on trust, but carefully and meticulously researched them as a matter of course. The Theosophical Society, with which he was publicly involved during the first dozen or so years of the twentieth century, relied to a great extent on traditional esoteric sources. However, he gradually replaced the Indian and other oriental terminologies in favour of his own, which were usually more descriptive and more acceptable to occidental esotericists, although a few terms and expressions have been retained.

One reliable and easily evident principle is that the number seven is closely associated with time, just as the number twelve is connected with matters of space. It comes as little surprise, therefore, to learn that these numbers are involved with the evolutionary process of the development of humanity as well as the Earth itself. As full details are to be found in Steiner's book *Occult Science* and the numerous courses of lectures he gave in amplification of its contents, only the most necessary features will be dealt with here, and should be considered in the light of other factors mentioned throughout.

Esoteric teachings posit seven great Earth-evolutionary stages, each one interspersed with a period of quiescence or *pralaya* passed in a state of dissolution. Here is a reminder of the whole schema:

(1) *Old Saturn*, when the foundations of our present physical-material body were laid by virtue of the outpouring of their own nature by the Thrones, or Spirits of Will. The characteristic 'element' was pure heat.

(2) *Old Sun*, when the life-principle in the form of the etheric body was added to our physical constitution, thus engendering our basic corporeal nature. The Old Saturn period was recapitulated, and air was the added element.

(3) *Old Moon*, when our astral nature was added after periods of recapitulation of the states of the previous evolutionary stages, and the elements condensed to form fluids.

(4) This evolutionary phase is that of our present *Earth*, when the divine spark which characterizes the human ego was added, and a certain culmination point reached. For the first time each human being becomes a fully self-conscious individual, responsible for his or her own destiny, and with the capability of acting freely. The four kingdoms of nature of which human beings are in a certain sense an agglomeration are now present simultaneously, and our fourfold constitution of physical, etheric and astral vehicles, together with our 'I', is now established.

(5) The immediately pending stage of evolution is that of *Jupiter*, when by virtue of our having spiritualized our astral nature/sentient soul through the ennobling forces of our ego, our constitution as spirit-self will be established. Earthly matter will be replaced by a much finer substance.

(6) The following evolutionary stage will be that of *Venus,* when the environment will be even more rarefied. Our etheric body/intellectual soul will have been transformed into the purely supersensory organization known as life-spirit.

(7) The final stage of the development of the Earth and humanity is known as *Vulcan,* when ideally an important level in our overall progress will have been reached. The environment will be entirely spiritual, our physical body/ consciousness soul will be transmuted into spirit-man, and we shall be dwelling among the spiritual archetypes themselves, when our existence will be that of a spirit among spirits.

It has become customary for this plan to be set out somewhat as shown in the diagram (over page).

Significantly enough, the number 7 appears even within these seven evolutionary periods, in that each one consists of $7 \times 7 = 49$ developmental cycles, including the recapitulatory stages. In all, therefore, there are $7 \times 7 \times 7 = 343$ stages from the beginning of Old Saturn to the end of Vulcan, although this figure in human experiential terms is somewhat academic. Certainly, in terms of actuality this is the case, and it is interesting to reflect that the circumference of Old Saturn, as a 'globe' of pure heat, coincided with the present orbit of the present planet Saturn, that of the Old Sun to the orbit of the present Jupiter, and of Old Moon to that of Mars.

It is clear that we are now in our fourth evolutionary period, each one of which is neatly reflected in the present Earth evolution as the four kingdoms of nature and in our fourfold constitution, four temperaments, and so on. It can

COMPOSITE PLAN

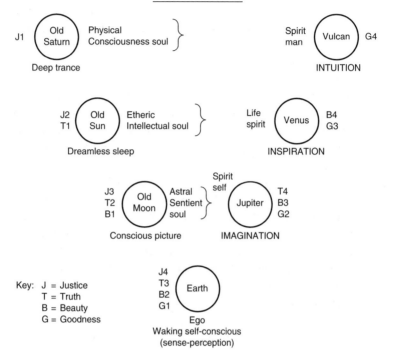

readily be seen that we as human beings represent a synthesis of the mineral, plant and animal kingdoms, with the added benefit of the individuality factor afforded by our ego. The remaining three cycles to be undergone involve the purifying and ennobling by our ego of the vehicles so far acquired until, at the end of the Vulcan period, even our densest member, our physical body, will have been spiritualized.

Those who achieve this shall, in biblical terms, experience the true 'resurrection of the body' and thus regain our purely spiritual state. Paul, in his first letter to the Corinthians (15:51–58) introduces his well-known passages on this eventual victory over death with the well-known words: 'See, a mystery I tell to you: we shall not all fall asleep, but all we shall be changed...' 'For it behoves this corruption to put on incorruptibility, and this mortal (body) to put on immortality... ' and so forth.

There is little need to mention our soul principles in this schematic arrangement because the soul arises as the result of the workings of the spirit in matter, and is therefore, strictly speaking and in ultimate terms, transitory. In present circumstances we make good and necessary use of our soul, in that it passes on to the spirit that which we experience by means of it in a physical-material environment. The soul members themselves, namely, sentient soul, intellectual soul and consciousness soul, arise as a result of the interaction of our ego with our astral, etheric and physical bodies respectively. The fact remains: we are indeed primarily spiritual beings.

Is our onward progress inexorable?

During our 'descent' via Old Saturn, Old Sun and Old Moon to the Earth, we were richly endowed with many qualities of which we were totally unaware at the time. We perforce existed under the auspices of the Hierarchies, and incorporated into ourselves their various 'gifts', having no choice but to accept circumstances as they were at any one time. We should always bear in mind that humanity truly belongs to the spiritual Hierarchies, as the Tenth, as Spirits of Love and Freedom. Human beings, alone among the higher Hierarchies from whom we have descended, are gradually maturing, however distant the goal, towards the accomplishment of our own impulses, fulfilling our own destiny, and achieving our own cosmic ideals.[2] Rudolf Steiner put the matter simply and concisely: The task of the Earth is to make human life possible ... and for us as free and independent human beings to attain to self-consciousness.[3]

The divine plan enables us to make use of our own powerful ego-forces, which are of course spiritual in nature, to 'ascend' via the Jupiter, Venus and Vulcan evolutions to universal consciousness whilst retaining our ego-consciousness. The gradual attainment of this consciousness is the realization, stage by stage, through Jupiter, Venus and Vulcan, of Imagination, Inspiration and Intuition respectively. As we have already seen, the fourth (present) stage of development as far as both the Earth itself and humankind are concerned marks the turning-point of time itself. Thus, having descended as deeply as is possible into matter, the task facing us now is to 'tie ourselves back', in the spiritual sense of *religare*, to our pristine divine origins. After suffering the Fall, the upward struggle back to a purely spiritual state, but this time in full consciousness, is our task ahead. Our progression through the final three future stages of further evolution, namely, those of Jupiter, Venus and Vulcan, is required to be done in a fashion which closely mirrors or relates to the three which preceded our present Earth evolution, but in reverse order, namely, Old Moon, Old Sun and Old Saturn.

Placed within a wider context, these facts fall neatly within a model which illustrates the whole process of human consciousness throughout the seven stages of the Earth evolution as follows:

Old Saturn	Deep trance universal consciousness (mineral)
Old Sun	Dreamless deep sleep consciousness (plant)
Old Moon	Dreaming or picture consciousness (animal)
Earth	Waking self-consciousness (human)
Jupiter	Imagination (conscious picture consciousness)
Venus	Inspiration (conscious sleep consciousness)
Vulcan	Intuition (spiritual or conscious universal consciousness)

We know from common experience that consciousness can be experienced at various levels, clearly categorized according to the conditions obtaining, which are characteristic of the seven developmental stages of both humanity, with which we are essentially bound up, and those of the Earth itself. As regards our present (fourth) stage, the general principle of this progression may be expressed as follows. Human consciousness has evolved from a state of extensive apprehension of the spiritual world combined with limited awareness of the material world to limited awareness of the supersensible world but extensive understanding of the material world. This is the progression humankind has undergone so far, and indeed still is undergoing as a kind of recapitulation of, but at the same time a transformation of, the states of consciousness obtaining on Old Moon, Old Sun and Old Saturn, but this time being fully aware during the process.

Our consciousness at the Old Saturn stage was nil, and the basic prevailing condition was that of Warmth, which is the outer manifestation of Love. Light, the spiritual counterpart of which is *consciousness* and therefore *thinking*, and by inference *wisdom*, arrived with the Old Sun evolution, and with it the principle of Life, as manifestation, according to plan, of the etheric forces. The level of consciousness on Old Saturn was that of deep trance, which nevertheless was universal in character; we were at one with the gods, but not aware of it. On Old Sun our consciousness was that of dreamless sleep, so that we were still not aware of what we were undergoing.

On Old Moon the astral element was added, thus establishing the foundations for future development in terms of sympathy and antipathy, and alternating states of consciousness in the manner of waking and sleeping, with its intermediate condition of dreaming. Here can already be discerned the evolving life of the soul, and conditions of increasing awareness of the outer world which was to develop at the stage of the Earth evolution we are now experiencing. We know from experience how unstable our sympathies and antipathies can be if they are not sufficiently managed or controlled. There is always the likelihood if not actual danger of error, prejudice, and misjudgement in our soul-life, and we must gradually attain, through the development of our aesthetic powers, to arrive at what is appropriate or 'true'.

This process is necessarily involved with our strivings towards moral rectitude, and the recognition of the powerful affinities between the archetypal powers of the so-called 'Eternal Verities', namely, Truth, Beauty and Goodness, to the extent that they do indeed represent a unity that is inviolable. Their powerful influences as fundamental archetypes in the evolution of humanity and the Earth will be discussed at some length in due course.

Some evolutionary parallels and comparisons

The four stages of evolution—Old Saturn, Old Sun, Old Moon and the Earth—representing as they do our physical, etheric and astral natures, are immediately apparent by the recapitulatory fashion in which the processes of growth and maturation of human beings in their seven-year stages occur. The infant stage spans the period from birth to the shedding of the deciduous teeth around the seventh year, when the etheric body is freed on all sides. From then until puberty, which now may occur as early as the twelfth year, but considered to be a nominal 14 years, when the astral nature is liberated, represents the period of childhood proper. The 'birth' of the ego occurs after the completion of seven years or so of adolescence, but which may actually occur at any time between the eighteenth and twenty-first year. Certain recapitulatory procedures with regard to the present embodiment of the Earth but on a smaller scale are apparent from the following table:

Cosmic aspect	Corresponding development stages		Relevant Epoch
Old Saturn	0–7	Physical body	7th Atlantean
Old Sun	7–14	Etheric body	Ancient Indian
Old Moon	14–21	Astral body	Ancient Persian
Earth	Birth of the Ego		
	21–28	Sentient soul	Egypto-Chaldean
	28–35	Intellectual soul	Graeco-Roman
	35–42	Consciousness soul	Anglo-Teutonic

This progression of the human race, from Old Saturn through Old Sun and Old Moon to our present Earth evolution on a cosmic scale, and its Earthly recapitulatory stages in terms of cultural ages, may well be considered as a kind of upbringing process according to a certain definite pattern, for certain specific purposes. As will become clear to those who are familiar with the principles of Steiner/Waldorf education, this pattern is essentially recapitulatory in operation and archetypal in both scale and accomplishment. Time and time again we see this principle, together with that of threefolding, in operation—so much so that it is possible to think quite concretely about their manner of application and reliability in anticipating results.

It was during the Old Saturn evolution that the foundations of our physical-bodily organization were laid, with a certain emphasis on rudimentary sense-organs. Rudolf Steiner went as far as to say that we consisted entirely of sense-organs,[4] and it comes as no surprise, therefore, that he characterized the infant also as 'wholly sense-organ'.[5] The behavioural mode during this time is imitation, when the young child copies the *actions* of those around them. In short, what you do, they do, and it is primarily the *body* that is involved in all action. Significantly, Steiner associates the employment of our senses with the nature of will rather than cognition, thus echoing the nature of the Spirits of Will who poured themselves out so as to give us our existence on Old Saturn and since.

During the Old Sun evolution the etheric body was added, and it was chiefly the glandular system that was developed. Connections with the plant world are plain; various secretions of human glands closely resemble the saps, oils, resins, nectar and other fluids which are of such vital importance throughout the whole plant kingdom, and the same term *gland* is employed. Ideally, childhood as such can be directly compared to 'the passionless plant', asexual in nature, and pure, artless and chaste. Without stretching the comparison too far, perhaps, we know that flowers, shrubs and trees, when subjected to careful cultivation by the discipline of the gardener, can be productive, agreeable and a joy to have around.

Similarly, the astral body was added during the Old Moon evolution, when our nervous system, albeit of a rudimentary nature, was incorporated. Our whole soul nature is virtually identifiable with that of our astral body, which with its sympathies and antipathies and mood changes generally is reminiscent of the waxing and waning of the present planetary Moon. The emotional and personality problems experienced by every adolescent is characteristic of this third seven-year life-period. Finally, during our present Earth evolution we have reached a certain culmination with the acquisition of our ego. True to recapitulatory pattern, it is 'born' at the traditional stage of majority, when the 'key of the door' to adulthood is procured. The corresponding time in evolutionary history had come when we human beings were freed from the tutelage of the gods and rendered capable of practising freedom of choice.

Rudolf Steiner was careful to point out that the accepted practice of following a line of intellectually based logic in a straightforward, one-directional, systematic pattern of thinking may indeed work out as anticipated, but things do not always conform to mere method. The history of orthodox science is littered with abandoned theories and rejected hypotheses—and that in the material world where causality is deemed to reign. It does rule there, of course, just as it does in the spiritual world, but materialistic thinking is one-sided thinking, and because it does not acknowledge supersensory factors of influence its path of knowledge is severely curtailed, and demonstrably liable to error.

As we have seen, the principle of recapitulation is firmly established within the evolutionary scheme. As a kind of law it is seen to be at work in countless processes involving both macrocosm and microcosm, and is accepted by both spiritual science and orthodox materialistic science. However, things are not always straightforward, and certain irregularities seem unexpectedly to assert themselves, resulting in apparent contradictions. However, on close scrutiny of the issues involved, we are frequently able to discern that in reality there exist no genuine inconsistencies. Quite often we encounter a definite, but orderly 'reversal' process where spiritual matters are concerned, which upon close examination make perfect sense. It is important to take the greatest care at all times, for as Steiner himself often stressed, our usual thinking habits may lead us astray. (See Chapter 7.)

In experiencing the spiritual world in direct ways, the principle of *reversal* is often seen to operate, and this can be very confusing indeed to those who prefer matters to be simple. A typical example is the so-called 'backward review' or 'retrospect' when, at bedtime, we carefully and pensively re-visualize, in reverse order, the most significant events of the day. Rudolf Steiner gave other instances of this reversal principle from time to time, and a few examples might help. He averred that a number, say 498, appears in the super-sensory realms as 894, and that commensurate with our ageing physical body with the passage of time, our etheric body grows younger. Similarly, when communicating with loved ones who have died, we have to bear in mind that messages that may be taken to emanate from the dead person may in actual fact emanate from ourselves, and vice versa.

Again, when we depart the spiritual realms and are born into the earthly environment, we already possess senses and sense-organs ready for us to use and develop. Conversely, when we are 'born' into the spiritual worlds at death we are entirely dependent on the degree and extent of spiritual development we have attained to on Earth for our ability to 'find our way around'. When we are conscious of the spiritual world, during certain periods after death, or whilst exercising spiritual perception, it is not we who 'move'; we attract things and beings of a spiritual nature towards us by means of our thinking activity, and they do actually *approach* us; we remain as it were quite immobile.

A good example of the kind of 'reversal' principle involved

was given by Rudolf Steiner in that whereas the evolutionary pattern of Old Saturn, Old Sun, Old Moon and the Earth established our physical, etheric and astral bodies and our ego were bestowed in that order, when the human embryo develops the reverse order of development obtains. That is to say, our blood-circulation, admittedly warmed and sustained by the mother, is the first system to develop, followed by the nervous system, the glandular system and lastly our superbly developed system of sense-organs nicely suited to earthly conditions.

In like fashion, on Jupiter, we shall be faced with the transformation of our astral body acquired during the Old Moon evolution, on Venus our etheric body gained on Old Sun, and our physical body which had its foundation on Old Saturn. This process takes place in reverse order of bestowal of our corporeal and soul principles. In passing, it is worth mentioning that our sense-organs, the foundations of which were laid on Old Saturn, are the last to be transmuted into pure spirit on Vulcan, our whole range of sense-organs having by that time been developed by the power of our ego into purely spiritualized organs of perception.

Similarly, during Earthly life, our physical, etheric and astral bodies during infancy, childhood and adolescence having been provided, our ego immediately sets to work in backward order to develop as far as possible our sentient, intellectual and consciousness-soul members. A parallel to this is that, during the seven post-Atlantean epochs, the fourth post-Atlantean epoch—the Age of the Intellectual Soul—exhibits a very special character in that it is pivotal, the central Age of seven, and marked by the endowment of our ego by dint of the Christ Event.

Expanding on these principles, the first post-Atlantean epoch—the Age of the Etheric Body—will be reflected in the coming seventh epoch, when our life-spirit member is due to be developed. The second (Persian) post-Atlantean epoch—the Age of the Astral Body—will be mirrored in the sixth post-Atlantean epoch when our spirit-self member will be developed. The third (Egypto-Chaldean) post-Atlantean epoch is being reflected in our own fifth epoch, the Age of consciousness-soul development. The fourth (Graeco-Roman) post-Atlantean epoch has no reflective influences, having marked the unique event of our being bestowed with the faculty of full ego-consciousness as a direct result of the incarnation, death and resurrection of a leading member of the Exusiai or Spirits of Form. As YHWH (Yahveh or Jehovah) or biblical 'Lord God' and leader of the seven Elohim (Old Testament), and the Christ as 'Word' (New Testament), He was responsible for the Creation. Thus the Earth and humankind, interdependent as they undeniably are, have reached the present stage in their evolution by means of 'co-operative' processes in accordance with the Grand Plan of evolution.

Thus, having gone through three evolutionary stages during which, stage by stage, our corporeal and soul-spiritual members were integrated by the workings of the spiritual Hierarchies, we have been brought to the point at which humanity faces a further three stages of development, as does the Earth itself. However, the successful realization of these stages will entail forces which have to be generated by human beings themselves in their 'upward' struggle towards the reattainment of a purely spiritual existence. In other words, we as purely spiritual beings who, starting as it were from Old Saturn on a mission to experience material conditions, find our goal on Vulcan, which may be described as a process of reunion with our origins—but at an enormously heightened level of development.

Some difficult issues discussed

Many people, in their sincere efforts to satisfy opposing arguments, attempt an uneasy compromise between God and belief in natural science, a dubious reconciliation between spiritual goals and seemingly mechanistic procedures. It is in any case difficult to avoid deterministic arguments, but a brief examination of relevant issues is warranted. If God has ordained the course of humanity, what of our free will? If evolutionary processes are accepted as inexorable, what of them then?

Regarding this question, Rudolf Steiner seems at first sight to have taken an uncomfortable stand between determinism and indeterminism. On the one hand his work concerning history, which concerns 'futures' as well as 'pasts' in the grand sweep of cosmic and human history, appears to indicate tendencies towards determinism. On the other hand, his assertions endorsing his self-engendered philosophy of ethical individualism as a genuine philosophy of freedom suggests that his attitude is undeniably indeterministic. Is reconciliation between these two opposing viewpoints possible? As ever in such matters, it is not so much a case of 'either/or' but of 'both/and'.

His contention was that it is perfectly possible for the Divine Beings who work from out of the spiritual worlds to provide a framework within which human beings may act freely, nonetheless within certain limitations. In other words, the 'Incalculable', having provided a 'calculable' environ-ment, now releases into it an uncertain mixture, namely, human beings with their calculable corporeal nature and their incalculable soul-spiritual nature. Our bodily nature is determined and calculable, composed of material substances which are subject to natural laws. Our soul-spiritual nature, together with our individual ego, as expressed in our diverse behaviours, is indeterminate and incalculable, composed of supersensory principles and subject to spiritual laws.

However, it might be said that our incalculable principles, notwithstanding powerful calculable influences, are widely regarded as representing a greater proportion of controlling influences during the course of our Earthly life than our calculable principles. Most people have an emotional bias towards libertarianism in the philosophical sense, but deter-ministic thinkers are capable of putting up a powerful case.[6] We must make of such issues what we are able.

Faced with the accusation of being a pattern-maker, Rudolf Steiner insisted that history, past and future, of Universe, Earth and Humankind is open to investigation by other spiritual researchers; they would merely confirm his findings. He stressed that the inherent orderliness which manifests itself in all spiritual laws is reflected in natural laws. However, he took a step further by contending that spiritual laws can be established after the same manner as natural-scientific laws, namely, by observation and deduction, and valid grounds for prediction are thereby provided.

He pointed out the difference between utterly reliable, even predictable, chemical reactions and his predictions concerning the coming destinies of ourselves and the world. He also outlined the differences between perception of the sensory and that of the supersensory; but both kinds of obtaining knowledge can be utilized with similar rigour and exactness, whether natural-scientific or spiritual-scientific. For instance, he maintained that, just as there is little chance that oxygen, hydrogen and sulphur will combine to make sulphuric acid at some future time in a manner contrary to the laws of nature, it is unlikely anything will occur in the spiritual life which is contrary to spiritual laws. Needless to say, the fact that spiritual laws are so little known and understood by natural scientists does not signify. To the objection that human freedom is rendered meaningless because events can, in a certain sense, be predicted, Steiner averred that the *conditions* under which natural laws and spiritual laws become operable depend on the human will.[7]

The distinction is a fine one, but it is clear that flexibility of circumstances must be allowed for if crude compulsion be not operative, which clearly it is not in either case. The will itself is not determined by law. What is determined by law is *that through which the will manifests as deed,* whether in circumstances natural or spiritual. It might be said that, just as the course of human life runs predictably through Shakespeare's seven ages of man, it would not be unreasonable to contend that humankind as a whole also has a definite course to run in developmental terms, in a definite order, in predictable stages. Certainly, the patterns concerning human and Earthly evolution that emerge from Rudolf Steiner's work give ample endorsement for its validity and value.

The Course of Western Civilization

We are on this Earth in order to gain freedom. The power to be free can only be found in the world of the spirit, the power to be free in heart and mind, and the power for freedom in our will. It is the goal of life on Earth to make human beings free and independent.[1]

Difficulties of recounting prehistory

It is impossible, and certainly futile, to attempt to delineate in fine detail the recapitulation of Old Saturn, Old Sun and Old Moon in past Earth evolution, but they can be applied in part to our present Earth evolution. Our primeval ancestors during these evolutionary stages had little or no concept of time, but in accordance with the general principle of recapitulation the three previous evolutionary stages have been duly repeated. We are now at the point in history identifiable as the fifth post-Atlantean epoch, also referred to as the Age of the Consciousness Soul, which commenced at around AD 1413 and is due to close at around the middle of the fourth millennium year at around 3573.

The grand westward thrust of Western civilization from the region of India, by way of Persia, Egypt, Chaldea and the Fertile Crescent area generally, Greece and Rome, and onwards to Europe, particularly to involve north-western European peoples, is of course fully known and appreciated by all historians. Naturally, this does not mean that contemporaneous civilizations and cultures elsewhere on the globe, and significant in their own way, are in any way to be undervalued. The significance of the Western series is that each Age succeeded the previous one in continuously progressive fashion, representing in turn the acme of sophistication during their particular span of existence. There can be no doubt about the supreme importance of this chain, for many of the impulses generated by these great civilizations over the millennia are still being developed in every country of the world today. Each of these Ages lasted for approximately 2,160 years, and correspond to one-twelfth of the so-called Platonic Year of 25,920 years, which fact is significant in itself.

Rudolf Steiner's pronouncements concerning the great sweeps of cosmic and human history are perhaps the more interesting because he spoke about the future as well as the past. He was careful to speak of probabilities and possibilities, and only rarely of certainties, as he was more aware than most people of the chances of humanity destroying itself and the Earth as well. He envisaged three main phases in human history and development: firstly, a primeval era when the World Spirit and the World Body worked as an undivided unity; secondly, a middle period, which includes our own times, in which they work as a duality; and thirdly a future epoch when the World Spirit will once again take up the World Body into its active working.[2]

During the first epoch, Steiner asserted, it would have been impossible to 'calculate' laws of nature in space and through time, as universal events were subject to the free intelligence and free will of Divine-spiritual Beings. 'Calculation' has meaning only for the second, present epoch, when laws of nature are able to be investigated and established; and only during this time are conditions provided which enable human beings to progress from a state of dim consciousness to one of clear self-consciousness, with free intelligence and free will of their own.

The present era is that during which human beings lose their former facility of spiritual vision, when conscious awareness becomes restricted to the world perceptible only by our physical senses. In this manner we are enabled to establish ourselves as free and independent beings. Of what lies in wait in terms of human destiny during the coming third epoch he had little to say, for obviously, the free will of autonomous individuals cannot be 'calculated'. It would follow from these contentions that 'history' as far as humanity is concerned can have meaning only *after* our full emancipation from direct divine-spiritual influences; that is to say, the middle epoch now current.

Rudolf Steiner made numerous references to historical stages both long and short, of various sorts, and in spite of the fact that he, knowing how easily confusion can arise, emphasized that they were made from different viewpoints, it is nevertheless not always easy to avoid such confusion. What many people find irritating, particularly historians and earth scientists, is his reluctance to put specific dates to some of the epochs and stages he delineated. From his own point of view, however, any attempt to pin down 'facts' concerning both temporal and spatial matters was meaningless and futile as long as the world-processes were 'incalculable', that is to say, before they became sufficiently stable for calculations in the shape of reliable natural laws to be rendered possible of establishment—and this, of course, was long before human beings possessed the necessary intellectual powers to enable such to be done. For instance, accurate observations of the heavenly bodies were made in Babylonian times which resulted in a geocentric conception of the world, but civilization had to wait for Copernicus before a heliocentric plan of our solar system, based on the necessary calculations, could be drawn up.

As well as positing the Incalculable-Calculable-Incalculable epochs, Steiner confirmed—from a different manner of approach which covers the first and part of the second of these three epochs—three prolonged periods which he referred to as Heavenly History, Mythological History and Earthly History. The first period lay entirely within the first incalculable epoch, when humanity as spiritual beings lived among the spiritual beings of the higher hierarchies, but bereft of individual intelligence and will. The second period, that of Mythological History, marks the time when Heavenly events were combined with Earthly events, the time of Gods and Heroes, when the affairs of human beings were 'managed' by divine influences which were more or less overtly manifested, and when the Mystery Centres became established. The third period, which encompasses Earthly history proper, commenced with the birth of the intellectual soul during the eighth century BC.[3]

Rudolf Steiner had much to say, again from different viewpoints, concerning the seven 'world-incarnations' or world-manifestations spanning immeasurable aeons: Old Saturn, Old Sun, Old Moon, Earth, Jupiter, Venus and Vulcan, the first three of which are history. Our present Earth evolution he divided into seven main periods, namely, Polarian, Hyperborean, Lemurian, Atlantean, and fifth (our own), sixth and seventh post-Atlantean epochs, each of which he subdivided into a further seven periods. Approximate dates and figures have been put to the Lemurian and later periods, notwithstanding the fact that they disagree with the findings of orthodox science. He was of course perfectly aware of this, yet he stubbornly defended his propositions from every kind of attack, as well as what dates he gave. The first three Earth-evolutionary stages are recapitulated in classic fashion, as follows:

1 Old Saturn recapitulated in the Hyperborean epochs
2 Old Sun recapitulated in the Polarian epochs
3 Old Moon recapitulated in the Lemurian epochs
4 Commencement of Earth evolution proper with the seven Atlantean epochs
5 Further development during the seven post-Atlantean epochs
6 Still further development during seven epochs
7 Yet further development throughout seven epochs

(There then follows dissolution into *pralaya*, a state of quiescence, in preparation for the Jupiter evolution, itself to be preceded by the appropriate recapitulatory epochs.)

Our ego becomes involved

The 'turning-point of time' occurred during the fourth (of seven) evolutionary stage of the Earth itself, that is to say during the fourth epoch, also of seven, in the course of the fourth (post-Atlantean) epoch, again of seven, which is also known as the Age of the Intellectual Soul. Coincidental with this turning-point was the appearance on the Earth, incarnated in human form, of an exalted spiritual Being belonging to the Hierarchy of Exusiai or Spirits of Form, and whom we acknowledge as the Christ. The various reasons and purposes of this Incarnation, which Steiner often referred to as the Christ Event, are too complex to be discussed in detail here, but the basic literature is extensive and readily available. Suffice it to remember that an important feature of the mission was the conferring of the faculties associated with the sense of ego on each individual member of humanity. We had arrived at last at the stage of experiencing a true sense of selfhood, and with it a greater awareness of our surroundings.

Rudolf Steiner's sevenfold configuration of the human being in his book *Theosophy* may be regarded as the definitive model, and this can be extended to indicate the developmental stages of the Earth as well:

1	Physical-material body	Old Saturn
2	Etheric or life body	Old Sun
3	Astral body	Old Moon
4	Ego or 'I', as soul-kernel	Earth
5	Spirit-self as transmuted astral body	Jupiter
6	Life-spirit as transmuted etheric body	Venus
7	Spirit-man as transmuted physical body	Vulcan

In the manner of a transitional step, the soul members—sentient soul, intellectual soul and consciousness soul—are developed, and a ninefold model of the human constitution is thereby also rendered valid, thus:

Spiritual members	Spirit-self	Life-spirit	Spirit-man
Soul members	Sentient soul	Intellectual soul	Consciousness soul
Corporeal* members	Astral body	Etheric body	Physical body

As we know, one of the principal tasks of the ego is the ennobling of the 'lower' vehicles that we have already acquired, namely, physical body, etheric body and astral body. The principle closest to the spirit-filled ego is so to speak the 'youngest' of these three vehicles, and the closest to it in terms of its essential nature is the astral body. This means that it is 'easier' to work on, resulting on the soul level of the generation of the sentient soul, the intellectual, rational or mind soul, and the consciousness or spiritual soul, which bear the particular influences characteristic of the intrinsic nature of the astral body itself as well as those of the etheric and physical bodies respectively. The connections of these soul members, each with its particular nature and function, are readily seen to be applicable to our soul-forces of thinking, feeling and willing respectively.

However, the work does not stop there, for with further refining of these soul members the three spiritual members are created, or prepared for in seminal fashion, namely, spirit-self from our astral nature, life-spirit from our etheric principles, and spirit-self from our physical constitution. Now it is these three spiritual members which, according to the grand scheme of things outlined by Rudolf Steiner, and touched on in the previous chapter, will be ripe for regular development in maturational terms during the coming three evolutionary stages of the Earth itself, and by implication the whole of humanity as well. These are usually referred to as

---

* This term may seem inaccurate at first sight, as only our physical body is a 'solid body'. However, these three are closely knit and interdependent when considered in relation to the spiritual members, all of which indwell the ego. The soul members are virtually the same as their corresponding spiritual members, with which they will eventually become identified.

the Jupiter, Venus and Vulcan stages, which will then complete the schedule of the seven stages mentioned in the same chapter.

It is at the present stage of the evolution of the Earth that its constitution—and again by strict implication that of the human physical body—is at its most dense. Accordingly, we have been obliged to develop bodily senses capable of apprehending an environment consisting in its outer manifestation as matter. However, the present situation whereby the spiritual world which exists behind all that is physical/mineral in nature and has become closed to us will be reversed during the impending stages of Earthly and human development. This will reveal itself as the acquisition by ordinary maturational processes which is at present regarded as more advanced, namely, the development of powers of supersensible perception of 'higher' worlds by means of esoteric training. In other words, the eventual unfolding by humanity of what is now known as Imagination, Inspiration and Intuition will take place during the evolutionary periods referred to earlier as Jupiter, Venus and Vulcan respectively by the agency of standard evolutionary processes.

The Platonic Year and its historical periods

The present time finds us about one-fifth through the fifth of seven post-Atlantean epochs, and this fact can be placed nicely into context by reference to the so-called Platonic Year. This represents a period of approximately 25,920 years, which is the length of time required for the sun to complete one retrogressive revolution of the Earth, passing before each of the twelve zodiacal constellations of the ecliptic in turn, and known to astronomers as the precession of the vernal equinoxes.

These twelve constellations give their names to the twelve 'signs' of the zodiac, each of 30°, with which they must not be confused, and with which they do not exactly coincide. This arrangement is often regarded with some misgiving or suspicion, irrespective of the fact that they are seen to 'work'. Thus each *sign* represents a period of 2,160 years (25,920 divided by 12), each degree approximating to 72 years (72 × 360° = 25,920). The sun, according to this configuration, is now before the *sign* of Pisces, the Fishes, which it entered in 1413, the approximate date of commencement of our present fifth post-Atlantean epoch or the Age of the Consciousness Soul, and on its retrogressive path will enter the sign of Aquarius, the Water-bearer, in approximately 3573, so heralding the sixth post-Atlantean epoch.

The actual symbols used for the zodiacal signs amply repay close study, for they contain valuable pointers to a clearer understanding of their meaning and significance. Bearing in mind that the human body has by long tradition been interpreted in terms of animals and other signs that feature in the zodiac, we may justly contend that we are indeed made in the image of God. Cosmic forces originating in the direction of the constellation Aries are responsible for the formation and function of the head. Similarly, Taurus influences the throat and larynx, Gemini the arms, shoulders and lungs, Cancer the rib-cage as a whole, Leo the heart, Virgo the lower abdomen and particularly the womb in women, Libra the hips, Scorpio the sex organs, Sagittarius the thighs, Capricorn the knees, Aquarius the lower legs, and Pisces the feet. The following diagram will help put the historical Ages in relationship with the zodiacal signs (*not* the constellations). The retrogressive movement of the sun is anti-clockwise, and our present 'position' in terms of this heavenly timepiece has been marked at approximately 22° of the sign of Pisces, the point reached by the sun after the 600 or so years that have elapsed since 1413.

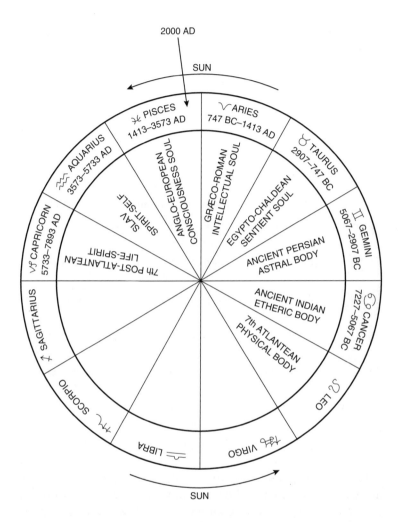

2000 AD

SUN

PISCES
1413–3573 AD

ARIES
747 BC–1413 AD

AQUARIUS
3573–5733 AD

TAURUS
2907–747 BC

ANGLO-EUROPEAN
CONSCIOUSNESS SOUL

GRÆCO-ROMAN
INTELLECTUAL SOUL

SLAV
SPIRIT-SELF

EGYPTO-CHALDEAN
SENTIENT SOUL

GEMINI
5067–2907 BC

CAPRICORN
5733–7893 AD

7th POST-ATLANTEAN
LIFE-SPIRIT

ANCIENT PERSIAN
ASTRAL BODY

ANCIENT INDIAN
ETHERIC BODY

CANCER
7227–5067 BC

SAGITTARIUS

7th ATLANTEAN
PHYSICAL BODY

LEO

SCORPIO

LIBRA

VIRGO

SUN

Stages of development during the present epoch

Rudolf Steiner was an outstanding historian in his own right, and his system of regarding history as subject to certain powerful cosmic, spiritual and other influences implicated a certain factor of necessity or inevitability with regard to his approach to it. Needless to say, the whole question of cosmogenesis and universal and Earthly history bears little

relation to the beliefs of orthodox cosmologists and geologists, who are in the habit of constantly revising their
figures. Interested readers are referred, apart from Steiner's
own work on these themes, to important work by other
authors.[4]

For further convenience, these historical periods are set
out in linear fashion:

Sign	Approximate dates	Historical epoch	Principle under development
Leo	Before 7227 BC	7th post-Atlantean	Physical body
Cancer	7227–5067 BC	Ancient Indian 1st post-Atlantean	Etheric body
Gemini	5067–2907 BC	Ancient Persian 2nd post-Atlantean	Astral body
Taurus	2907–747 BC	Egypto-Chaldean 3rd post-Atlantean	Sentient soul
Aries	747 BC–AD 1413	Graeco-Roman 4th post-Atlantean	Intellectual soul
Pisces	AD 1413–3573	5th post-Atlantean Anglo-Teutonic	Consciousness soul
Aquarius	AD 3573–5733	6th post-Atlantean Slavonic	Spirit-self
Capricorn	AD 5733–7893	7th post-Atlantean	Life-spirit

During our present Earth evolution the appropriate manner of perception to which we have evolved is thoroughly
cognitive in nature and character. We have been equipped
with a full range of twelve senses by means of which we are
rendered capable of apprehending the sense-world in which
and by which we live and evolve.[5] All human beings seek to
gain knowledge of, and strive to understand, the material
world in which we find ourselves, relying on the evidence of
its manifestation and presentation of phenomena, and the
various laws of nature thereby revealed. We all possess this
obsessive urge to understand what goes on in and around us,

and if such understanding is to be complete and entire it must include perception, insight and comprehension, not only of the physical/material world but also of the spiritual world which lies behind it and from which it proceeded. It bears reiteration that in the course of the present Earth evolution human consciousness has evolved from a state of extensive vision into the spiritual worlds combined with limited awareness of the sensible world characteristic of prehistoric humanity, to limited awareness of the supersensible world but extensive clarity of vision and understanding of the material world which is evident today.

The outstanding characteristic of the present Age of the Consciousness Soul is that 'through our consciousness soul we penetrate the secrets of the outer world as human beings endowed with knowledge and cognition'.[6] But for full understanding of our environment, of the detailed knowledge of the material world, which is being accumulated at an ever-accelerating rate by research scientists, must be added the wealth of indications given by spiritual science concerning the complementary world of the spirit. It was a matter of historical necessity that Rudolf Steiner be incarnated at a time when materialism was very close to its nadir, but there has been as yet scant recognition of his work by orthodox scientists.

However, the seeds he sowed are sprouting sporadically, but to what extent they will grow and bear fruit is still a moot point. He maintained that as an activity of the human spirit, working in complete freedom in respect of thinking, individuals would eventually come to realize the reality of the supersensory worlds, and furthermore gain in knowledge and experience of them, thereby to confirm the spiritual nature of the universe in its origins and manifestations. However, it must be said that the willingness or readiness of the vast majority of civilized individuals of sufficient motivation and capability to grasp spiritual science is relatively infrequently met with, and growth is slow.

Bearing all these issues in mind, it is fortunate that most of

Steiner's findings are readily available in print, notwith-standing the fact they are virtually ignored by contemporary thinkers and the general public. However, it is more than likely that if his many indications continue to be ignored, particularly those concerning social, educational and eco-logical issues, the prospects and actualities for communities worldwide will continue to deteriorate. An almost certain consequence of this will be that, when social turmoil and strife reaches unmanageable proportions and intellectually arrived at 'solutions' are seen manifestly to fail, his indica-tions will be seized upon in desperation as a last resort, and taken seriously. His earnest efforts to introduce the notion of the Threefold Social Order failed, and his warnings that the continuing slide into barbarity would not be checked if radical changes were not implemented (along the lines he indicated)[7] have gone unheard. The instability evident in social, economic and political and ecological affairs on both national and international levels since the First World War is gradually increasing. He gave perfectly valid and well-argued grounds for such indications, obtained as they were directly as a result of his researches into the spiritual realms, and seen, in the absence of prejudice and preconception, to be perfectly sound and reasonable.[8]

However, there are already signs, even among those who acknowledge the value and integrity of his accomplishments, that his work is being regarded increasingly as a body of belief rather than knowledge. There seems still to be the widespread notion, even among those who are reasonably well acquainted with his findings, that what he expressed was opinion, albeit informed, rather than truly representative of actuality. Fortunately, his undeviating insistence that the formulation of a genuine *science of the spirit* is already achievable by those who take the time and trouble to study his indications and methods of arriving at them is never-theless still regarded seriously by a minority of individuals who strive to put them into practice.

The way forward

The progression of the universal human race, from Old Saturn through Old Sun and Old Moon to our present Earth evolution, can be seen as a kind of upbringing process according to a certain definite pattern, for certain definite purposes. An archetypal pattern is clearly seen to have been operating over the aeons, centuries and decades. This pattern is essentially recapitulatory in operation and archetypal in both scale and execution, for time and time again we see archetypal, recapitulatory and threefolding principles in operation, thus enabling us to think concretely about their manner of application, and to anticipate appropriate results with reasonable confidence.

For example, Rudolf Steiner's life clearly shows a seven-year rhythm, and is readily identifiable with the history of the founding and promulgating of anthroposophy itself. More-over, it is barely conceivable that he did not make deliberate efforts to arrange his activities accordingly.[9] He himself referred to the whole body of wisdom-knowledge that he formulated from his own supersensory investigation and research as a genuine science of the spirit, a truly spiritual Being to which he gave the name *Anthroposophia*.[10] Its developmental processes exhibited a similar rhythm to those of human beings, and he drew the attention of Society members to this fact in a lecture in Stuttgart on 6 February 1923.[11] This corresponds to the periods 1902–09, 1909–16, and 1916–23; at the end of 1923 he took on personal responsibility for the leadership of the newly restructured General Anthroposophical Society, which after 21 years' growth and development had indeed come of age.

From the very moment that the German Section of the Theosophical Society was founded in 1902, Rudolf Steiner rightly perceived that the theosophical movement was virtually incapable of initiating any practical activities, whereas he already knew that the Being Anthroposophia was capable of bringing forth 'children' in the shape of organizations and associations which could do useful work in the world. In a lecture given on 25 October 1915 he mentioned this parallel rhythm in a somewhat whimsical fashion by reference to the anthroposophical movement acquiring its second teeth.[12]

These three periods of development also correspond to the three great educational ideals which inspired the western stream of civilization and culture over the last few millennia, and indeed to the whole educational process of all children who receive a genuinely Waldorf education. In Greek times the ideal was the *gymnast*, when education was by means of bodily movement, wrestling, athletics, dance and suchlike, whereby the *will* is primarily engaged. During the Middle Ages the educational ideal was the *rhetorician*, who by means of the faculty of speech and understanding of the human being's soul-qualities could influence people by way of *feeling*. In modern times the ideal is the *doctor*, the learned individual who passes on what knowledge he or she has acquired by means of spiritual endeavour through *thinking* and use of the intellect. The ideal of the future is the *universal human*, whose educational goal is to hold the other three in balance by the powers of the *ego*, thereby providing a comprehensive education for the whole human being.[13]

4

Truth, Beauty and Goodness as Archetypal Principles

*Mankind descends through the realms of mineral, plant, ani-
mal and human, and ascends through the moral, the aesthetic,
and the realm of truth and knowledge. In this way, humanity
participates in that wonderful stream of being that develops as it
flows through Saturn, Sun, Moon and Earth, and onwards
through Jupiter, Venus and Vulcan. There are lesser streams
that overlap and unite in man, creating the separate forces he
needs in the course of his development. These are granted to
humanity from out of the deep impulses that rule the cosmos.*[1]

The 'Eternal Verities'

The Eternal Verities of Truth, Beauty and Goodness are
readily identifiable as the three great and lofty ideals which
have inspired leading figures in succeeding civilizations over
the millennia. Many thinkers throughout the centuries have
regarded them as virtually synonymous with one another,
and Rudolf Steiner maintained that they were indeed a unity
in ancient times but have become differentiated with the
passage of time. Far from being mere abstractions, they are
concrete realities which bear witness to the knowledge of our
far ancestors concerning human nature as it stands in connection with the universe—and this he was able to confirm
from his own spiritual investigations.

Certainly, they all bear archetypal characteristics and significance, and in human affairs they have been gradually
made manifest over time as Science, Art and Religion
respectively. In what follows it is helpful to bear in mind the
observation made by Rudolf Steiner that individuals who do
not strive towards the acquisition of truth and truthfulness,

and goodness and high moral standards, are in actual fact in a position of doing positive harm to their fellow humans, whereas those who make no effort to appreciate beauty in all its manifestations succeed in depriving only themselves of whatever benefits such realization brings.

We know that the laws that operate in the spiritual realms are utterly moral, where nothing in the nature of untruth, deceit, lies and so on is permitted to exist. Steiner contended that our feeling for truth is directly connected with the consciousness we experience of our bodily nature, which was fashioned in the spiritual worlds before our birth with the active co-operation of our individual guardian angel and other, more exalted, spiritual beings. The subtle connections between our physical vehicle and our sojourn in the realms of Truth prior to our arrival on Earth are preserved during our lifetime only if our whole existence is lived with regard to high moral standards. This of course is by no means easy, but truth should nevertheless be upheld and maintained as an ideal. At the same time we do well to ponder the fact that our bodily organization cannot 'lie' to us, but remains unswervingly true in sickness and in health.

Common as 'white lies' and untruthfulness in general are in everyday life, and which are for the most part disregarded or treated lightly, we may be sure that penalties, albeit self-administered, will be exacted during our passage through the spiritual realms after death.[2] Any intellectually conceived attitude towards untruthfulness, which is a matter associated with our spiritual nature rather than our urge to rationalize everything, including our lack of moral standards, must not be allowed to pass. With every excursion we make into the shadow-world of lies, deception and so on, we sever one more thread which connects us with the spiritual world we left at birth; indeed, our very consciousness of the existence of this world diminishes with every severance.[3]

Our etheric body also has its origins in the supersensory worlds, and although orthodox science suspects that such a body or 'field' of formative forces actually co-exists with our physical body, it is unable or unwilling to countenance its reality. Rudolf Steiner averred that a sense of such reality is strengthened by our experience and appreciation of beauty, pointing out that the extent of such acknowledgement signifies the measure of our true humanity. A genuine feeling for beauty also renders possible the maintenance of our connections with the higher worlds we left prior to our birth. This is difficult to sustain in today's aesthetically barren cultural scene, in which we are surrounded by much that is ugly, uncouth and tawdry.

Steiner consistently stressed that art is vital for the development of our soul-spiritual nature generally, and that it constitutes an essential means of acquiring knowledge. In connection with this he said: 'From out of the imperishable world resounds the faculty of imagination acquired by humanity as a substitute for spiritual vision, and manifested by individuals in perishable form.'[4] The mission of art, therefore, is to provide for the transition from primitive artistic impulses right through to future spirituality. The great value of art lies in the fact that spiritual perception withdraws ever more in proportion to the extent that the outer sense-world gains ground and the human ego develops. Art can therefore be seen as a counterbalance to the intellectualism which is regarded as a necessary adjunct to scientific research and technological development. From all this we can appreciate that the pursuit of Truth, as of Beauty and indeed Goodness, represents three different aspects of the same range and scope of human endeavour.

Sir Herbert Read's assertion that 'the purpose of art, which is the communication of feeling, is inextricably confused with the quality of beauty'[5] had been iterated by others before him, including Steiner. Elsewhere, Read restates the Greeks' conviction:

> beauty is moral goodness, is really a simple truth. The only sin is ugliness, and if we believed this with all our being, all other activities of the human spirit could be left to take care of

themselves. That is why I believe that art is much more significant than either economics or philosophy. It is the direct measure of man's spiritual vision.[6]

It comes as little surprise to learn that goodness, from certain viewpoints,[7] is involved directly with the astral body, which is the vehicle for our feelings. The exercising of genuine goodness must, almost by definition, engage the heart-forces, and that kind of fellow-feeling which is sincere and direct, and bears the stamp of self-denial. Deeds prompted by this essentially human quality are given without thought for any reward. Those stirrings of the emotions which result in the urge to extend the hand of friendship and non-possessive, unconditional love and regard represent the essence of goodness. The physical and etheric bodies, as comprising our corporeal nature, cannot be experienced in the direct manner in which our astral body, our soul-nature, is experienced by our ego. Our very use of language reveals much in this regard. We employ expressions which indicate that we *possess* our *objective* corporeal members, but that we *are*, in a very real sense, our *subjective* soul and spiritual principles. For example, we 'have' a cold, headache, blister or rheumatism, but we 'feel' or 'are' happy, angry, jealous or miserable, honest, decent or unselfish as the case may be.

To simply *be* good in the abstract is not of much use or benefit to anyone; it is by actually carrying out free acts of loving-kindness and mercy that the attribute of goodness is validated. All acts of will entail a sympathetic flowing over into, a certain uniting with, the beneficiary of such good deeds, and this bears implications of a positive nature for the doer's life after death. Genuine goodness is expressive of high standards of morality, and is fully consonant with those obtaining in the spiritual worlds.

Apart from experiencing the appropriate satisfaction resulting from those deeds of loving solicitude whilst in kamaloka, there will be other very significant 'rewards'. According to the strength of our capacities for compassionate, altruistic love and the will to action whilst on Earth, we are able after death to draw forth from our soul the necessary strength for its creative powers to be activated. The result is the awakening and gradual development of what Rudolf Steiner described as 'soul-light', which is available for the purpose of illuminating the spiritual realms, and which 'streams through, shines and glitters through everything'.[8] By reason of the presence of this soul-light, thoughts, which with their spirit-filled content abide in this supersensible environment, are thereby rendered graspable and comprehensible.

Similarly, for us to have striven to seek after truth during our life on Earth—and thus by implication wisdom—by proper exercising of our powers of thinking is also of great importance. Our understanding of the soul and spiritual worlds which we pass through during our life after death largely depends on our appreciation of truth during our sojourn on the physical plane. Just as we grow after birth into the realms of the astral (animal), etheric (plant) and mineral (physical) realms of the earthly world, so when we enter the heavenly realms after death we encounter the moral sphere (Goodness) during kamaloka, the aesthetic sphere (Beauty) whilst passing through the seven regions of the soul world, and the sphere of wisdom (Truth) during our progress through the seven regions of the spiritual world proper. It can therefore be seen that we are enormously advantaged if we are subject to a wholesome socialization process and an education that pays proper regard to the three Eternal Verities as manifested in religion, art and science respectively. In Rudolf Steiner's own words:

> Man becomes human by descending to the physical plane and growing into the mineral, plant and animal realms. After death, we ascend again. Then something similar happens from a spiritual point of view: in the spiritual world something happens that resembles the growing into the three kingdoms of physical existence on earth. As a human being grows into the spiritual worlds he is received into the realm of morality, the aesthetic realm, and the realms of wisdom, or truth.[9]

Thus we can see that we lead as it were a double life. Our spiritual nature dips down into the world of matter at our birth and consequent existence on Earth, where we strive, as beings who contain within ourselves the attributes of the three 'lower' kingdoms, to employ their gifts in scientific, artistic or religious ways as appropriate. Obversely, we strive to reach up into the realms of spirit by dint of our Earthly strivings to bring to actuality the three great ideals of Truth, Beauty and Goodness that have been implanted in us during the course of our evolution so far. So, just as our physical organism connects us with the mineral, plant and animal realms, so the moral sphere, the aesthetic sphere and the sphere of wisdom connect us with the forces of the spiritual world. A simple table makes this clear:

Earthly	Mineral kingdom	Physical body
realms	Plant kingdom	Etheric body
	Animal kingdom	Astral body
Heavenly	Kamaloka	Goodness (morality)
realms	Soul world	Beauty (aesthetics)
	Spiritual world	Truth (wisdom)

As we have seen, the Verities have great significance during the life after death in that what is experienced during kamaloka, and our subsequent passage through the soul world and spiritual world, depends largely on whatever activities we took an active part in during our earthly life. The connections between these and the physical, etheric and astral vehicles which they inhabited also become clear.

During kamaloka it is Goodness that is the criterion, expressed as love in action, as deeds of altruism, that is put to the test of morality, and more or less painful conclusions arrived at. During the passage through the seven regions of the soul world, a certain balancing out of the feelings of sympathy and antipathy is undergone, for these two factors are of paramount significance to us during our Earthly sojourn. The correspondences between what kinds of emotion or sentiment were enjoyed or endured on Earth are also made irritatingly or encouragingly plain to us for our ultimate advantage and benefit. Upon entering the spiritual world proper we are put to the test concerning our familiarity with concerns of the spirit rather than matter, and experience accordingly what is our due in terms of enhanced or diminished consciousness. There we are surrounded by readily accessible wisdom, and the nature and being of Truth is revealed.[10] In connection with this, Steiner confirmed that in the spiritual world it is especially important to have developed this feeling for truth of what has been experienced in the physical world.[11]

Truth, Beauty and Goodness in cosmic history

Towards the close of his lecture *Truth, Beauty and Goodness* on 19 January 1923, Rudolf Steiner stated:

> To be true is to be rightly united with our spiritual past. To sense beauty means that in the physical world we do not disown our connection with spirit. To be good is to build a living seed for a spiritual world in the future. Past, present, future—these three concepts, as they play their part in human life, assume far-reaching significance when we understand the concrete reality of the other three concepts: Truth, Beauty, Goodness.

Upon the basis of this observation it is reasonable to suggest that the order in which the three Verities, Truth, Beauty and Goodness, are placed is not arbitrary, but justifiable on an archetypal scale—as naturally appropriate as Past, Present and Future, and as we have seen, this order is respective and matches perfectly. Now in his lecture course *The Riddle of Humanity*, Rudolf Steiner makes comparisons on a cosmic scale, in a manner reminiscent of the axiom 'As above, so below', which is important enough to be listed as a useful subject for daily meditation.[12]

It is not surprising that in Christian ethics the idea of Justice has, as in philosophical ethics, three main referents:

(a) God's justice as righteousness or uprightness, that is to say, absolute justice; (b) the right ordering of life among human beings, namely, social justice; and (c) the virtue of justice as an individual attribute. In this arrangement can be divined the same elements that we are now discussing, although in different terminology. How could it be otherwise in the light of the findings of spiritual science? We know that relative justice is all that can be achieved at present, but it is good to know and be able to appreciate the *ideal* of justice. Needless to say, perhaps, profane laws devised by human beings may be just or unjust, but the archetypal principle of justice remains inviolable.

In his cosmic scheme, which encompasses the evolutionary stages of development of both humanity and the Earth itself, Rudolf Steiner introduced a fourth 'Eternal Verity' in the notion of Justice in addition to the other three. Oddly enough, perhaps, he had comparatively little to say about this aspect of human experience, but if approached in a meditative way, certain thoughts present themselves which seem reasonable and fitting. Now each Verity, as far as its development in terms of the human race is concerned, undergoes a series of four distinct, consecutive stages, each series being allocated as appropriate to four Earthly 'incarnations'. They are so arranged that they all overlap at one particular time, and that is during our own—Earthly—stage of evolution, as follows:

Stage of evolution	Justice	Truth	Beauty	Goodness
Old Saturn	1			
Old Sun	2	1		
Old Moon	3	2	1	
Earth	4	3	2	1
Jupiter		4	3	2
Venus			4	3
Vulcan				4

From this arrangement it is plain that the Verity of Justice worked on humanity for three Earth-incarnations during the aeons that we human beings lacked conscious realization of what was actually happening. It is only now, whilst it is active in its final stage, that Justice has, as it were, reached a certain maturity with regard to our mode of consciousness. Our instinctive attitudes towards the idea of Justice are as profoundly felt, if not more so, as those we direct towards the notions of Truth, Beauty and Goodness. These are deeply ingrained in the human constitution, and are obviously of a moral and therefore soul/spiritual nature.

It is also worth mentioning that Justice is listed among the now traditional seven 'natural' virtues, namely, Prudence, Fortitude, Temperance and Justice, consisting of a quadrivium of cardinal virtues, which figured in Plato's thinking and are therefore of pre-Christian origin. Faith, Hope and Charity comprise the trivium of theological virtues, expounded so elegantly by the apostle Paul, and are widely understood to have been bestowed on humanity by a special grace of God. Rudolf Steiner expands on the four cardinal virtues in the light of spiritual science in lecture five of *The Riddle of Humanity*. The theological virtues are discussed towards the end of Chapter 6, but for present purposes we need to discuss only Justice, which reaches its culmination during the Earth evolution or 'embodiment'.

With the whole concept of justice is associated a keen appreciation of what constitutes 'natural justice'—fair play, equality, the same standards for everyone in human affairs, and so on. We don't need to be taught what justice is—and it is by true instinct in the sense of its having been built into our very constitution that we know it when we see it in action. The ever-expanding system of administering justice through local, national and international courts, and the burgeoning legal industry give ample evidence of the universal human love affair with matters legal if hardly the principle of justice itself. Moreover, justice is the very factor by which karma or self-created destiny operates on the physical plane, with all its complicated interrelationships, the arranging and activating of the appropriate and compensating events, and so on. It comes as little surprise, therefore, when we learn that Justice as an archetypal being has been present within us in our evolutionary progress ever since Old Saturn.

Justice and the law of self-correction

Rudolf Steiner mentions the 'cosmic law of self-correction of all existence' in a lecture given in 1909[13] but understandably enough does not expand on it. He is obviously referring to karma or self-created destiny, and this in turn can justifiably be related to Old Saturn, which marked the introductory stage of the principle of Justice. On another occasion he said: 'If we seek for forces having something of the nature forces of Old Saturn, we have to go to the laws of our personal karma ... Deep in the background of our being lies our invisible personal destiny. How this invisible personal destiny is determined comes under the rules of Old Saturn laws.'[14]

Moreover, relations can also be realistically established with our present planetary Saturn, as part of its function is notably that of repository of all memories concerning past events in both material and spiritual worlds. This role of preserving cosmic memories has obvious inferences for the workings of karma, which itself entails enormous effort on the part of the higher Hierarchies on humanity's behalf. Saturn 'represents the moral justice of the universe in its highest aspect'.[15] It is therefore entirely fitting for the principle of Justice as the extra 'Verity' to have been involved with our genesis during the Old Saturn evolution, and so built into our very constitution from the very beginning, and indeed into the whole of nature, whose laws needless to say are utterly moral.

As we know, the 'nature forces' referred to in the quotation above were largely expressed through the medium or factor of *warmth*, living warmth, and this attribute is with us today as the heat of our blood, bodily warmth. Another significant fact is that our ego lives, so to speak, in the heat of our blood, that 'very special fluid' which is fundamental to life itself. Obviously, it is our ego that is engaged in every aspect of how we live our lives, and which in the final analysis is responsible for all our deeds and actions. Here again is a subtle connection with karma, the literal meaning of which word is *work*, and by implication the forces generated by our karma expressed in what we *do*. By reason of the causal nature of our self-created destiny we deal out our own justice according to our individual deserts.[16]

However, as a kind of obverse to Justice, stern and impartial, we have the quality of Mercy, of compassion, grace and charity. Mercy is usually regarded as the prerogative of God or divine powers, and the grace of God, and indeed of the Lord Jesus Christ, is a common theme in biblical writings. Needless to say, the whole concept can be seen to be clearly related to the free sacrificial deed of the Christ and His whole mission to the Earth, which was anticipated long before the actual Event. The role of Christ as the Lord of Karma, taken up as it was during the final phase of the establishment of Justice during the present Earth evolution, thus appears to be entirely appropriate. Hence all faith is justified, and all knowledge sanctified.

The principle of Justice as a stern and relentless equalizing agent is deeply rooted in many peoples, notably the Hebrews, who still hold fast to the ethics of demanding a tooth for a tooth and a scrupulous levelling of scores. It certainly is as though the principle of Justice was actually woven, or increasingly 'programmed' into our very being during the Old Saturn, Old Sun and Old Moon stages. With the enormous enhancement of our ego-consciousness by the Christ Being during the present stage of Earth evolution, Justice may now, as it were at the point of culmination, be brought up into our full consciousness and be transmuted into *conscience*, as we shall see. It is noteworthy that the consummation of the ideal of Justice took place virtually at the turning-point of time, when Mercy in the shape of the sacrificial deeds of the Christ superseded the old order. Furthermore, the new Covenant (or Testament) establishes this on a universal scale. That it also forms the basis for a truly universal Christian religion, still demonstrably in its embryonic stages, is evidence of this. Christ is the Lord of Karma and is therefore responsible for its implementation now and into the future.

The very principle of Justice itself is totally in accord with that of karma or self-created destiny. The axiom 'As above, so below' appertaining to cause and effect is operable in both spiritual and material worlds, for the latter originated in the former. The laws obtaining in the spiritual world are wholly moral, and the so-called laws of nature, as a product of that world, were therefore obliged to take on its consummate and unequivocal character. On our path to perfection we are responsible for our own progress on our own efforts. It seems that only when we prove ourselves to be worthy of them are the blessings of the spiritual worlds bestowed on us as a gift of grace.

We know that our personal destinies are entirely self-created, but these have only been subject to being generated since we were endowed with enhanced ego-strength, and have been responsible for creating our own karma. When we lived entirely under the protection and direction of the Beings of the Spiritual Hierarchies this was not possible. We received the first glimmerings of selfhood during the late Lemurian epoch and the beginnings of the Atlantean Age, but it is only since the Christ Event that we have acquired complete freedom in our life of soul and spirit.

As we know, the rudiments of our physical body were originally formed during the Old Saturn period, as a consequence of the Thrones or Spirits of Will pouring themselves out as it were in sacrifice. This is perhaps more easily understood when we recall that our physical vehicle consists of matter, which is 'hardened' or solidified *will*, and which can be readily associated with the factors of resistance, gravity and so on. The first stage of Goodness manifests at the fourth or Earthly stage in the evolution of humanity, the development of which constitutes a major task which, during the next four 'upward-striving' states of the Earth evolution, reaches its final stage during the period of Vulcan.

Justice and conscience

The connections between the Eternal Verities and our soul-activities of thinking, feeling and willing respectively are readily discernible, but those with past, present and future are perhaps less obvious, apart from the manner in which Rudolf Steiner links them.[17] The archetypal principle of Justice was touched on earlier, but it is worth repeating that the four stages it goes through reach their culmination with our own Earth evolution. It is reasonable to contend that it was already present in the consciousness of humanity as exemplified by the biblical account of Job, who certainly gave the whole concept of justice a thorough airing. We shall become increasingly able to bring to it the forces of our ego, but in terms of implementation it shows obvious links with the principle of conscience. Biblical scholars place the book of Job at around the fourth century BC, and perhaps it is no coincidence that it was at about that time that Aeschylus, Euripedes and other Greek dramatists were also then occupying themselves with problems thrown up by the 'human condition'.

It is common in modern times to regard conscience almost entirely in terms of psychology, and rather as the result of our being somehow 'trained' during our formative years of infancy and childhood and thus part of the general socialization process. This presupposes influences of an external origin, whereas a true appreciation of conscience originates in our inner being and is entirely self-generated. There is a widespread tendency to emphasize the feelings of guilt which are associated with the workings of conscience, and therefore rationalize it along these lines, usually in negative terms. This is of course partly true, but it is far from being the whole story. With the decline of the influence of religious teachings, moral standards have also degenerated, and in the present moral climate, with crime rates becoming ever higher, there is increasing public alarm concerning the fact that children do not seem to know the difference between right and wrong. However, all this is part of the problem of living in the Age of the Consciousness Soul, with egotism, ambition, and crass materialism as norms.

In terms of Earthly and human history, the principle of Justice was the very first to be implanted into the very constitution of human beings right at the outset, at the time of Old Saturn. It is therefore as 'old' as our physical body, and it is true that we feel that the ideal of fairness, upright-ness, natural justice and righteousness, in the sense of conforming to divine or moral laws, lies at the very root of personal and social behavioural standards. Feelings of guilt or shame arise unbidden in us when we know very well that unfair actions on our part are unjust, unethical and inequi-table. Strict impartiality is a significant factor where the principle of justice is involved, and symbolic of this is that many artistic representations of Justice appear blindfolded. Hence, too, the ubiquitous presence at sporting, athletic and other competitive events of umpires, referees and so on.

The general pattern of advancement in cosmic and human affairs seems to imply that development takes place in four stages or phases, and this corresponds to the fourfold nature of the human being. In four successive epochs of Earthly and human evolution we find ourselves having been provided with our four principles, namely, physical-material, etheric, astral and an ego-organization, gifted to us during the Old Saturn, Old Sun, Old Moon and the Earth itself respectively. The remaining three evolutionary periods will be occupied by our managing, processing or otherwise developing these principles with their complete spiritualization as the goal. The pattern of one purely spiritual entity, namely, our real and immensely powerful 'higher' Ego which resides entirely in the spiritual worlds rather than its earthly counterpart, working on three previously acquired principles can be clearly seen to work in the case of humanity, and also in the case of the Being Anthroposophia itself. (See Chapter 3, pages 41–42.)

This arrangement works in parallel with the bestowal by the higher spiritual powers of Justice and the three Eternal Verities by neatly overlapping stages, as we have seen. It is clear that we have two 'given' or 'perfected' principles handed to us as finished products, namely, Justice and Goodness, the former spanning the 'downward' evolutionary stages, and the latter the 'upward' stages. Justice is so to speak 'imposed' on us *as Law*; it is present within our most intimate reaches as a predetermined propensity, an instinct which has been built into us by the archetypal spiritual powers. For Paul the Law is 'holy, just and good' (Romans 8:12), and the basis for all morality is 'righteousness' or 'uprightness', thus reflecting the nature of God Himself.

Conversely, in a kind of reciprocal fashion, just as Justice speaks to us and we respond or not according to our degree of acknowledgement of it commensurate with our progress along the path to perfection, so Goodness speaks as it were from within ourselves as an impulse for *moral deeds*, but only if we have rendered ourselves capable of doing so *in freedom*. The ultimate goal is goodness to all and for all, the common weal or *universal good*. It is significant that Goodness first manifests as an archetypal principle, at least as far as humankind is concerned, during our present stage of evolution, when we attain to a clear sense of ego, self and not-self, inner and outer.

It is as if, by attaining to the highest pinnacle of Goodness at the close of the Vulcan evolution, we shall have 'redeemed' the principle of Law as Justice, attaining instead to an enormously enhanced degree of 'ethical individualism'. In this process we shall be enjoying the assistance of our *conscience* in its function as a kind of counsellor, guardian and guide in the whole process. Ideally, this means that, ultimately, we shall not need the application of or reference to any external constraints. Our inner promptings of conscience will eventually become fully integrated into our nature and constitution.

The two central Verities, namely, Truth and Beauty, will reach their zenith at the close of Jupiter and Venus in turn, which is marked by their both having reached their fourth and final stages respectively. Goodness, with its close affinities with our ego, may only begin to be incorporated into our deeds and manifested on the Earthly plane at the appropriate stage of its—and our own—evolution. As Steiner asserted, we can only speak of goodness when there is a distinction between an inner and an outer world, so that goodness can obey the spiritual world or not,[18] and this is why Goodness as a Verity emerges in terms of human evolution precisely at the stage when our ego-consciousness is fully achieved.

Further matters of conscience

No one would deny that when our conscience is stirred so is our sense of justice. Indeed, it *is* our sense of justice (Latin *conscientia*—conscious of guilt). Taking the whole concept further, the concept of *rightness* is seen also to be related to conscience, and it is but a short step from that notion to that of *truth* itself, for what is true is bound to be right. Closely related to our experience of conscience is *shame*, when feelings of guilt arise as the result of our outer, public behaviour when it attracts the disapproval and moral condemnation of an impartial populace. In this respect it is noteworthy that the word 'conscience' does not appear in Old Testament scriptures, and that the Christ Impulse in the shape of Christian teachings found ready acceptance by peoples to the north and west of Rome long before the advent of our present Age—that of the Consciousness Soul— in the fifteenth century.

This consciousness of guilt—one might almost say of 'sinning'—is operative at both the level of our thinking, in that it is easily demonstrated that what is good for one is good for all, and at our level of feeling, in that we experience regret, remorse, and even sorrow on account of our wrong-doings. This points to our having achieved a certain maturity in our moral development, and may be related to the fact that it is during our present Earth evolution that Justice as an archetypal principle reaches its final stage, as indicated earlier. We ourselves are far from maturity in this respect, but we are at least already capable of appreciating the value of ethical probity in human affairs, and of acknowledging its value in society. It is by exercising our conscience that we are able to make ethical progress, and it is worth noting that Paul makes use of the word *conscience* no fewer than 22 times in his Letters, whereas it is employed on only eight occasions by other writers throughout the remainder of the New Testament.

It is clear, therefore, that we must have acquired our sense of conscience comparatively recently in the history of humanity, coming at approximately the same time as the endowment, by virtue of the Christ Event, of the enhancement of the realization of our ego. Symptomatic of the manner in which our former ego-consciousness was so dim and unresolved is the fact that the personal pronoun 'I' was not expressed, as now, by employment of a separate word, but was contained within the appropriate verb. Both the ancient Greek and Latin languages gave evidence of this, in that *eimi* and *sum* respectively were used for the expression 'I am'. Indeed, all personal pronouns were similarly integrated into the construction of all verbs, thus demonstrably identifying the individual agent(s) with whatever action was effected. Thus our acquisition of a genuine ego-consciousness can be seen to have occurred during the Age of the Intellectual Soul, which ran from approximately the time of the foundation of Rome in 747 BC until approximately AD 1413.

The previous Age, that of the Sentient Soul, otherwise known as the third post-Atlantean epoch, had centred on the so-called Fertile Crescent which comprised Egypt, Babylonia, Chaldea and neighbouring Middle East civilizations. As development of the sentient soul is integrally bound up with the astral body, it still retained features of this cultural period. For example, communion with divine principles lingered on, as evidenced by widespread reliance on dreams (typified by the story of Joseph and Pharaoh), visions and prophecies for guidance on Earthly matters. Humanity was not yet self-reliant.

We begin our training in self-reliance

With the onset of the fourth post-Atlantean epoch the main thrust of civilization gradually shifted westward to involve the peoples of Greece and Rome, and the development by them of the arts and architecture, as well as social values, law, politics and so on is well chronicled. This was the time of the great Greek dramatists who, like the philosophers, mathematicians and others, caught the spirit of the time and sought to express themselves accordingly. Rudolf Steiner identified Aeschylus as the individual who, through his plays, and particularly the character of Orestes, was instrumental in making clear the workings of conscience as a personal quality or attribute, and which later was to develop throughout civilized humanity.[19]

It is significant that it was during this fourth post-Atlantean epoch that, by reason of the Christ Event, humanity acquired this enhanced sense of egohood. The ego is so to speak 'at home' in the intellectual, rational or mind soul, for thinking as a spiritual activity is closely associated with the ego as agent. It is an initiator, originator and inaugurator *par excellence,* as deeds lacking forethought and toil without deliberation is fruitless endeavour. Contemporary myths at this stage of civilization denote a humanizing of the gods, a virtual loss of connection with the divine worlds, and in consequence a further diminution of communion with them, which resulted in the eventual abandonment of oracles and similar means of divination and revelation. This was characterized by the intense and fruitful cultivation of our mental powers which showed a greater degree of individuality.

There inevitably arose a greater reliance on individual human performance and ability; thinking became more creative, more consciously reflective, and hence more differentiated. The putting into concepts of what had hitherto been expressed in imagery and revelation marked a great step forward in the intellectual life of western civilization. There is general agreement with Bertrand Russell, who, in his *History of Western Philosophy*, placed the true birth of philosophy with Thales in the sixth century BC, as did Rudolf Steiner before him.

It was characteristic of the Greeks and Romans that they wished to create a realm within the sense world which expressed as closely as possible the spiritual within the physical, and this is strikingly exemplified by the near-perfection of their artistic and architectural masterpieces. Significant of this period, which ran to the time of the Renaissance, or more exactly 1413, was the spread of Christianity throughout Europe. An effective vehicle for this was the Roman Empire with its extensive and efficient network of communications, and the consequences were far-reaching and profound.

The fifth post-Atlantean epoch or Age of the Consciousness Soul is set to run until approximately the year 3573. Now Steiner pointed out that whereas the heightening of ego-consciousness by people everywhere at that time by virtue of the Christ Impulse was undergone *belatedly* by those involved in the Egypto-Chaldean civilization, it   was experienced *prematurely* by the peoples of Europe, particularly those of northern Europe. It is clear that the birth of *conscience* as a factor in human history coincided with everything we associate with the Christ Event in terms of our ego-consciousness. Actually being *conscious* of the moral quality of our own conduct or intentions, together with feelings of obligation to refrain from doing wrong, is an essentially inner experience belonging exclusively to our most intimate soul-spiritual nature.

In addition, the strength of our will and urgent desire to act freely, according to our own standards and not to those imposed from without, had taken on fresh impetus. Hitherto, in the course of our development throughout the stages of Old Saturn, Old Sun and Old Moon, we were not able to act freely, being then under the direct influence and authority of divine powers responsible for our guidance and progress. However, with the bestowal by Christ of our ego-hood at the turning-point of the Earth evolution as well as that of Time itself, we are now set, as individuals in our own right, to take charge of our own moral development on the road to perfection. This notion ties in directly with the introduction by Rudolf Steiner of the philosophy and principles of *ethical individualism* as being in full accord with historical necessity.[20]

The Eternal Verities and Society

*We will turn our attention today to the three domains which
actually comprise all human activity on Earth: to the thoughts
through which we endeavour to assimilate* Truth *in the world;
to feelings in so far as in and through our world of feeling we
endeavour to assimilate the* Beautiful; *to our will-nature, in so
far as we are meant to bring the* Good *to fulfilment through it.[1]*

Two basic questions addressed

Where educational philosophies are at issue, the question
What am I as a person? is more significant than *What is
important for me to know?* Rudolf Steiner was of course by
no means a lone voice who supplied the obvious answers to
these questions, which are being echoed by many mainstream
educationists today who realize the futility and wrong-
headedness of dictatorial State edicts which lay down every
conceivable rule as to pedagogy, curriculum and didactics at
all levels. Protestations of practising teachers are largely
ignored, and school governing bodies are conspicuous by the
presence in their ranks of amateurs who take pride in having
been convinced of the rightness of government policies by
sheer weight of media publicity concerning copious statistical
data, which obligingly serve to provide support for the
fallacies peddled by these means.

The fact remains that the governments of most western
countries have no genuine educational philosophy. At the
very most they concoct various policies largely based on the
demands of employers and educational establishments at
tertiary level who connive with the various public examining
bodies to provide whatever tests that serve to sort out the
achievers from the non-achievers. Whatever policies there
are are arrived at on an *ad hoc* basis, using the latest research

on problems of achievement in a frenetic race to provide the best 'centres of excellence' in whatever occupational/ utilitarian, cultural, athletics or sporting field. The latest researches are supplanted by the very latest findings, which are sooner or later abandoned in favour of further changes based on the newest analytical investigations by career academics, intellectual through and through, whose main function is to power this endless carousel.

The Verities and civilization

The three Eternal Verities of tradition are fundamental and powerful influences in human culture and civilization, and as forces of archetypal dimensions they figure large in the whole process of socialization and education, whether people are consciously aware of it or not. Acknowledgement of the immense importance of these ideals necessarily precedes attempts at their realization in terms of everyday life. The tendency nowadays is to concentrate on Science as seeking for knowledge in order to reveal truth in Nature, and its acquisition has mainly to do with the intellect. Emphasis is therefore placed on the importance of cognitive skills to the detriment of Art and Religion. This trend is readily observable in the educational practices followed in most orthodox schools and colleges. There seems also to be growing evidence of further shifts towards the regarding of education as representing merely a training ground for the specific purpose of obtaining employment in a shrinking job market.

There seem to be variances concerning what Steiner had to say about the emphasis to be placed on teaching strategies as appropriate to the stages of maturation in children's development, but as is usually the case they are more apparent than real. In the light of our discussions the following passage is in every respect relevant, serving to indicate fitting foundations for a genuine philosophy of education:

[We should be] able to bring it about that our children grow in the right way into the *true*, which they bring with them as an inheritance from the spiritual world; that they then unite themselves aright with the *beautiful*, and finally that they learn also, here in the world of sense existence, to be *good*, for it rests with them to impress the good upon the world into which they have come. It is a downright sin to speak in an abstract way of the true, the beautiful and the good without showing clearly and practically how these three are related to the different ages of childhood.[2]

A religious mood permeates every attitude of the child from birth to the shedding of the deciduous teeth; an artistic perception of the world is unconsciously sought and cultivated by the child from the second dentition to puberty; and after that time the adolescent, with rapidly developing intellectual powers and objectifying approach to the world, is by nature a scientist. Thus are the three main fields of human endeavour reflected in the three ages of childhood. The first period of the child's life is spent with the unconscious assumption 'the world is moral'. The second period is spent with the unconscious assumption: the world is beautiful', and only with adolescence comes the possibility of discovering 'the world is true'.

The word beauty derives from the Middle English words *beaute* and *bounte* (goodness). Etymologically, therefore, goodness may be regarded almost as being synonymous with beauty, and indeed it is clear that there are very close relationships among all three Eternal Verities. What is also consistently clear is that Beauty maintains its central position between Truth and Goodness, at the same time being heavily influenced by both principles. This arrangement is reminiscent of the position of the human soul with regard to the human constitution, as supportive of both spirit and body alike. We attain to Truth mainly by way of exercising our (antipathetic) thinking faculties, whereas we practise Goodness through our (sympathetic) willing faculties. The intermediary function of Beauty maintains a balance between these two by dint of its main connection with feeling, and feeling must be present before any attempt to attain to knowledge be possible, and must precede acts of love and devotion expressed through our powers of willing.

The paramount attribute of Beauty and its manifestation—which of necessity is the expression of the spiritual through and by means of the material—is that it unfailingly serves to uplift the human soul. This is its main and essential criterion. Beauty is thus seen to be the educator *par excellence* of the human spirit via the aesthetic experiences of the soul, which serves to establish and preserve *harmony* and equilibrium between Goodness and Truth as well as providing a bridge between the two, thus linking them and furthering the influences of both, making up a genuine trinity—three in one and one in three.

Rudolf Steiner contended that all genuine works of art issue from spiritual sources, from which all knowledge flows.[3] He maintained that an education involving artistic activities and exposure to aesthetic experiences is vital for the development of the human ego. Moreover, art acts as a counterbalance to the intellectualism which is a necessary complement to all educational procedures, especially scientific research and technological development. From all this we can appreciate that the pursuit of Truth, as of Beauty and indeed Goodness, represents three different aspects of the same range and scope of human endeavour.

Steiner repeatedly urged everyone who sought further to expound spiritual-scientific truths, principles and tenets to regard every issue from many viewpoints, so as to arrive at as true a picture of it as possible. Another perspective of the whole complex area of Truth, Beauty and Goodness was stated by him as follows:

However, in neither of these worlds—the world in which we are unconscious in the sleeping state, nor the world in which we are half-conscious in the dreaming state—in neither of these worlds do we find goodness. There, the beings, right from the beginning, were predetermined by wisdom. In them one finds the powerful weaving of wisdom, one finds beauty. But if, as inhabitants of Earth, we reach these beings and want to understand them, it will be pointless to speak of goodness where they are concerned. We can only speak of goodness where there is a distinction between an inner and an outer world, so that goodness can obey the spiritual world or not. In the same way as the state of sleep is assigned to truth, and the state of dreaming to beauty, the waking state is assigned to goodness.[4]

With reference to (c) in the table on page 68, we see that Truth is asleep in the infant; but by means of its progression through Beauty during the dreaming stage of childhood, it may attain to Goodness when the astral body 'awakens'. In complementary and reciprocal fashion, the infant, having emerged from worlds of highest morality and radiating Goodness, may also by way of Beauty attain after puberty to Truth, when the astral body 'awakens'.

We have seen earlier that Beauty embarks on its first stage during the Old Moon evolution, that is to say, when the etheric forces introduced by virtue of the impulses characteristic of the Old Sun evolution enliven and organize the unformed and barely differentiated primitive physical body acquired on Old Saturn. After the Old Moon evolution the 'gestating' astral body is 'born' at the 'pubertal' stage of both Earth and human being, when the 'educational' process through Beauty towards Truth, now in its second stage (which corresponds to that between the shedding of the milk teeth and puberty) is ready to proceed in earnest. Hence there is no valid contradiction in the table, as may appear at first sight.

In his lecture *Truth, Beauty and Goodness* which Rudolf Steiner gave on 19 January 1923, he connected Truth with the physical body, Beauty with the etheric body, and Goodness with the astral body. These various notions are here brought together in relationship to one another:

	(a)	(b)	(c)	(d)
0–7	Truth	Goodness-will	Truth-sleeping	Physical body
7–14	Beauty	Beauty-feeling	Beauty-dreaming	Etheric body
14+	Goodness	Truth-thinking	Goodness-waking	Astral body

(a) *Education for Adolescence*, lecture 8, 19 June 1921
(b) *Man and the World of the Stars*, lecture 5, 16 Dec 1922
(c) 'Measure, Number and Weight—Weightless Colour', 29 July 1923
    (in *Colour*, Part II)
(d) *Truth, Beauty and Goodness*, lecture, 19 January 1923

It can be discerned at once from the table that the only
stable or constant factor is that of Beauty, with its well-
known connections with our feelings and the dreamlike
consciousness associated with them. The variations concern
Truth and Goodness, but there is no contradiction in their
relationships with the other factors; it is apparent rather than
real. As we perceived from a different point of view in the
previous chapter, just as we grow into the Earthly world after
birth we enter the Heavenly worlds after death in corresponding fashion: the realm of Goodness or morality
(kamaloka); of Beauty (aesthetics) in the soul realm, and
Truth and wisdom in the spiritual world proper.

Thus there is a close parallel between these three stages
and those obtaining during infancy, childhood and adolescence, with the development of the physical body, etheric
body and astral body respectively. There are also correspondences between these stages and the evolution of the
Earth itself: the foundations of our physical nature were laid
during Old Saturn, those of our etheric body on Old Sun, and
of our astral body on Old Moon. After the adolescent stage
the ego is added, and this occurs during our present Earthly
stage of development—the recapitulatory correlations are
plain.

With regard to the development of all life, all being, even
that of the Spiritual Hierarchies, Rudolf Steiner stated:

Humanity evolves to ever higher stages of development from out
of its own forces. We can look up to sublime beings who,

dwelling in exalted spiritual heights, become ever mightier. How do such beings become greater? At first they need something, require something from the world. Later, they develop so they can give something. *The fundamental spirit and purpose of development is that one proceeds from taking to giving.* We can find an analogy in human development between birth and death. Children are helpless and must accept help from individuals in their surroundings. But gradually, they outgrow this helplessness and become helpers in their own circle. The same is true of the grand span of human development in the universe.[5]

This principle has a direct bearing on the apparent contradiction in the table between column (b) and the other three columns. Infants 'take' all they can from their environment in simple and utter trust that they will receive what they need, and this of course is Goodness. This is an unconscious process. The Verities of Truth and Beauty do not in the least concern them at that stage; but after puberty the pursuit of Truth in full consciousness, by reason of their newly born astral body, is entirely appropriate. Rudolf Steiner asserted that moral impulses enter the human organism through the head, thus implying that *the person must be awake.*[6]

The fact that 'truth flows directly into the etheric body, lives with thoughts in the etheric body' is in no way contradictory, but fits neatly into the overall picture. We know that the etheric body 'gestates' during infancy, becoming free on all sides during the seventh year. It is during this time that the child bears within itself the assumption that the world is true, and this is why the process of imitation is so effective. After the shedding of the deciduous teeth the child is mature enough to assimilate Beauty and everything that is aesthetic in nature. Aesthetic impulses originate in the spiritual world, and work directly on the astral body, which gestates from then until puberty, then to be born, ready to assimilate Truth in full consciousness. With the birth of the ego the adolescent is capable of acting in Goodness to approximately the same degree that morality was imbibed during infancy, at least to start with. Therefore, 'In Truth, man opens his etheric body directly to the cosmos—initially, it is the etheric part of the head. In Beauty, he opens his astral body directly to the cosmos. In the sphere of morality—Goodness—he opens his 'I' directly to the cosmos.'[7] The relationships involving the stage of entry of each Verity, namely, at the Old Sun, Old Moon and Earth evolutionary periods, and thus by implication those of the development of humanity, are again underlined here. The 'Verity' of Justice was of course implanted into our nature at the Old Saturn stage.

We are of course now living in the Age of the Consciousness Soul, and by inference we have the task of rendering ourselves as *aware* as we possibly can in every respect we possibly can. This means, as mentioned earlier, that we must be 'awake', and this implies being *watchful*—and perhaps even prayerful—for moral impulses from the spiritual realms entering our consciousness. It is no coincidence that Rudolf Steiner appreciated the value and importance of our being thus watchful and observant, recommending as earnestly as any New Testament contributor that we remain wakeful and watchful, directly echoing these words of Mark 13:37, 'And what I say unto you I say unto all, Watch.'

He gave a weighty reminder of this in what he asserted to be a 'no more esoteric saying' than the words 'The Christ is watching us', as quoted in *Verses and Meditations* (page 222) taken from a lecture he gave on 1 November 1915. Undeniably, it is our duty also to be watchful of the Christ. It is difficult to escape the impression that here Rudolf Steiner is giving a strong indication that this factor of watchfulness is a reciprocal activity. He warned against the 'drowsiness of soul' present in his time, but nowadays it is widespread, being energetically promoted in the form of entertainments, amusements and similar diversions so liberally provided by means of Ahrimanic gadgetry such as television, video, electronic games apparatus and suchlike. The ever-watching but inattentive, inert, indolent 'couch potato' is a creature typical of our times, and serves as a warning to everyone of the dangers attending this particular state of oblivion.

Right thinking: afterthought and forethought

The whole matter of right thinking in the interests of establishing the truth of things provides a rich source of argument for scholars and philosophers, and it need hardly be said that it requires sensitive impartiality and considerable powers of discernment, not to mention awareness. Rudolf Steiner often stated that we all possess an inherent capacity for sensing truth regardless of our standards of intelligence or education, and he was amply qualified to speak on the subject, providing useful insights into the whole question of right thinking in these words:

> To think properly it is necessary to bring together in thought the actual events and then wait to see what emerges ... there is truth not only in what is said but also in what is done. The Cosmic Word ... can only be understood if we extend its meaning as widely as possible ... this Cosmic Word really vibrates and undulates also in everything that happens, in every event that takes place.[8]

Obviously, *right thinking* must be in accord with the validity of the premises representative of the facts involved. A fact by very definition must agree with the truth, and if truth is integral to what happens, then the event qualifies as *right action*, so that Truth and Goodness are seen to be reciprocal, complementary and in essence interchangeable. Steiner pointed out that, in the usual course of events and in general, truth is arrived at by thinking, which belongs to the past as accomplished activity, thus arriving at a conclusion after whatever mental labour is necessary is due largely to what he termed *afterthought*.[9]

This is how orthodox science approaches the establishing of truths; conclusions are arrived at inductively or *a posteriori*—after the event. In our strivings to attain to truth we must of course be totally objective; there is no room for egotism or self-indulgence of any kind. Thus, in a word, by seeking after Truth we train ourselves to be unselfish, and impartial in our judgements. But Steiner goes further than this, declaring that 'truth is our leader to concord and human understanding, and prepares the way to justice and love'.

If Truth is to be attained to, we must maintain a selfless attitude. There is no room for mere opinion, and the adoption of egotistic attitudes. Truth is not necessarily a matter of attaining 'cold fact'. On the contrary, experiences undergone on the path to discovering and maintaining the Truth are themselves training in altruism, and inclinations to concord and harmony, and even peace. The Truth always establishes a common ground which brooks no contradiction, as in the case of mathematical truths; there can be no dispute about them. Hence there can only be agreement, and thus complete lack of opposition or antagonism. All this is sufficient to justify the contention that the seeking after Truth, the love of Truth, also extends to love for the whole of Creation.[10] In a very real sense, therefore, Truth may be equated with Goodness, because the latter attribute cannot exist in the abstract. It cannot remain merely as an ideal, an exercise in mental appreciation of the desirability of Goodness as a theoretical principle which can never be realized; it is necessarily realized in deeds as love in action.

The apostle Paul maintained that 'the truth shall make you free', and reflection has shown that the selflessness that leads to full recognition of truth permits the necessary factor of detachment to become established. Acquisitive, egotistical people whose constant wish is to satisfy their own desires by 'owning' other people as well as material goods—and all for their own indulgence—merely succeed in building up pain and woe for the future, when they will be required, by one means or another, to be separated from the objects of their attachment.

With regard to the attainment of right thinking, Rudolf Steiner argued convincingly that there are two ways of arriving at a truth: one by reason of *afterthought*, as we have just considered, and the other by *forethought*. Of the latter he said:

> The one and only proof of truths resulting from forethought lies in their actual verification. Not being derived from observation they cannot be demonstrated in the same way as truths resulting from afterthought. Their confirmation must be sought in the actual facts of life. There is thus a vast difference between the first and second kind of truth. Strictly speaking, the second is grasped primarily through spiritual activity and then verified by external observation.[11]

He consistently showed that spiritual truths, and knowledge supersensibly acquired, are in complete and necessary agreement with the knowledge that can be gained from the world of the senses; that is to say, by scientific methodologies applicable to both spiritual and material worlds alike. Only thus can the various truths coalesce to form part of a Truth that is anywhere near absolute.

Truth, Beauty and Goodness as active agents

In the usual threefold model of the human soul, feeling occupies the field of tension between thinking, which in nature is antipathetic, and willing, which is sympathetic. As Steiner emphasized, the essential task of education is to bring the soul-spiritual members (ego and astral body) of children and young people into harmony with their corporeal members (etheric and physical bodies). Put another way, as hinted earlier, it consists in successfully integrating the subjective nature of the pupils and students with their objective nature. Gradually, under the influence of right education, the feeling-willing behaviour characteristic of young people is transformed into the thinking-willing propensities of adults. With the subjective element of feeling thus having played its part in the generating of objectively purposeful thinking which, as incentive or motivation, precedes any action taken or deed performed, true rationality attends the whole event. Thus we can see that *ethically valid* thinking results in deeds which proceed from willing the *truly good.*

It can be seen from the table earlier that there is some variation as to the deployment of the Verities in relation to their connections with other factors involved, notably the stages of human development. What we must bear in mind at all times is that the archetypal forces of Truth, Beauty and Goodness are all present as long as the three principles of spirit, soul and body of the child remain in a substantially undifferentiated state; that is to say, until approximately the third year. Until then, it has no conscious appreciation of any of the Verities. The already highly developed spirit is asleep in the head; its powers of comprehension, reasoning and other intellectual capabilities are nil at this time. The partly developed soul is dreaming in the head, and it is compara-tively soon that the infant develops a primitive feeling life, which develops apace. The body is awake only in the limbs which are being constantly exercised during the child's waking hours, for this is the stage at which the child learns its motor and co-ordination skills, and this with increasing proficiency.

As we know, a freeing process rather than complete differentiation occurs at the appropriate maturational stage: the child's 'own' rather than hereditary *physical* body at seven or so years of age, when its facility for arriving at truth by thinking is made partially available for development by means of thinking. This proceeds gradually, but ideally in concert with the life of feeling, which engages the child's *etheric* organization, and all teaching should embrace that which is of the character and nature of beauty, namely, by creatively artistic methods which accord to a state of dreaming in terms of consciousness. At puberty the astral body becomes free, and with it a greatly enhanced capability for discovering truth in the world by purely intellectual means of constructing thoughts and concepts unhampered by any subjective sentiment.

Now Rudolf Steiner describes the inability of orthodox science 'to describe man in a waking state, by ascending through beauty to goodness'.[12] This is the process that has just been described, and it equates to a diminution of instinctive or unconscious wisdom at the cost of increasing clarity of waking consciousness, for this is a spiritual law. To quote him further:

> [The child] works on itself by means of a wisdom which is not within it. That wisdom is mightier and more comprehensive than any conscious wisdom of later years. The higher wisdom becomes obscured in the human soul, which in exchange receives consciousness.[13]

However, the whole matter is capable of being examined from another point of view, which is equally valid, and moreover serves to explain the apparent contradiction in Steiner's statements. The Verity of Goodness is a special one in many ways. It cannot be reached by the intellect alone, or by exercise of the feelings alone. It comes so to speak as a gift-package straight from the spiritual world, and it necessarily operates as morality, as moral law which human beings may observe or not, according to choice. Morality as a 'subject' cannot be taught; rather it can be instilled by example, or 'awakened' by reasoning, which has certain definite connections with Beauty. (See Chapter 4.) But Goodness *per se* is of little use unless it is put to some purpose, namely, that of carrying out deeds and actions for the benefit of others. Virtue may be its own reward in certain circumstances, but if this entails self-love it is of no use to anyone, most definitely not ourselves. Rather, the adolescent is at the point where he or she is able to *think* that which they have previously willed and felt.[14]

If, as ideally it should be, such thinking is imbued with the forces of Goodness and Beauty induced by wholesome imitation during infancy, and educated through creatively artistic methods under a kindly authority during childhood, the performance of moral deeds by adolescents and adults, their actually doing good in the world in full consciousness, is thereby rendered more likely. In effect, the whole matter is paradoxical rather than contradictory.

All this can be seen to support the notion that Goodness is not only an unconscious attribute present in the infant, but also that it bears strong relationship to the fully developed astral body, as mentioned by Steiner in *Truth, Beauty and Goodness*. This is also seen to be chronologically valid, for this is the order in which we develop in successive stages, as mentioned earlier. The Truth, if we possess it, makes us free, gives us choice; the Beautiful is also the Good, and as all true art necessarily conforms to the standards of Beauty, we are in effect left with no choice other than to strive towards the Good. The corresponding fields of operation expressive of human culture are Science, Art and Religion respectively, and as these were once a unity, and will become so again, so may we embrace Truth, Beauty and Goodness all as an integrated whole:

> To be true is to be rightly united with our spiritual past. To sense beauty means that in the physical world we do not disown our connection with spirit. To be good is to build a living seed for a spiritual world in the future.[15]

It is worth mentioning at this point that Rudolf Steiner associated Truth with the physical body, Beauty with the etheric, and Goodness with the Astral body. Now the foundations of our physical or mineral body plainly lie with Old Saturn, and this means that without the life-giving properties of our etheric organization it remained lifeless and inert. This is why, in terms of life-endowed entities, any material body must be animated by taking up, or being taken up by, forces of a formative nature, and this characteristic resides in the etheric. In other words, for any object to be designated as an Earthly organism, it must consist of both physical-material and etheric body, as exemplified by the plant kingdom and bestowed during the evolutionary stage of Old Sun together with *light*, which is so necessary for most vegetative life.

However, as we know, the essential characteristic of etheric forces is their anabolic or growth-inducing powers, and this entails and encompasses the additional capacity for creating forms. This power of *forming* is not only confined to animate and, by implication, physical-material organisms capable of metamorphosing, but it can also be applied to what might be imagined as thought-substance manifesting as mental processes. Thus we are able to form ideas, notions, and concepts, to analyse or synthesize patterns and paradigms, form judgements, arrive at conclusions, make plans in the fashion of mental pictures in the memory or imagination, and so on.

All these operations necessarily engage our form-making, creative powers, and these are precisely those which are required in order that works of art be produced. The plastic-formative arts spring readily to mind in this respect, and they invariably entail the taking up of physical-material substances and imbuing them with artistic qualities and properties. In this regard the etheric forces tend towards the sensory realms of matter. On the other hand, they may be employed rather with that which engages the soul-nature, namely the musical-poetical arts, thus tending 'upwards' to the astral rather than 'downwards' towards the physical-material. Paintings, sculptures, drawings and suchlike take on existence in *space*, whereas music, song, eurythmy, prose and poetry writing and reading, and recitation and drama occur mainly through *time*. Obviously, formative forces of numerous kinds are bound to be employed in creative fashion in all such artistic expression, thus 'ensouling' matter in many and diverse ways. It can therefore be claimed with considerable justification that the etheric principle is closely related to Beauty in all its forms, both plastic-formative and musical-poetic.

Evolution and the Verities

As we have seen, the Verity of Truth reaches Stage 3 for the benefit of humankind during the current Earth evolutionary period. Currently, too, Beauty will attain to Stage 2, whereas Goodness will have accomplished Stage 1, corresponding to an introductory level. Also at this time the principle of Justice completes Stage 4, its final one. This configuration is an interesting one, which repays study and reflection, for there is a certain inevitability about the whole arrangement of all four fundamental principles.

Our earlier discussion concerning conscience gave affirmation to Rudolf Steiner's assertion that this important human attribute revealed itself in terms of experience and consequent behaviour during the Age of the Intellectual Soul, which also saw the dramatic event which he referred to variously as the Christ Impulse, the Mystery of Golgotha, the Christ Event or similar. Without the enhanced sense of ego, the imparting of which formed an integral element in the whole significant occasion, together with the new sense of ethical responsibility which was born in humanity at that time, the gift of conscience would not have been possible. Moreover, it is reasonable to submit that had this not been so, Rudolf Steiner would not have found it possible to promulgate his philosophy of *ethical individualism,* which is incorporated in his overall epistemology concerning freedom, when he did.

The present Age is that of the Consciousness Soul, when human ego-consciousness has been strengthened and intensified even more, and this as a matter of historical necessity. We now possess—or should, ideally at any rate—a keener sense of what is good and what is evil, what is moral and what is not, and this as a result of the development of the human conscience. Inevitably, the element of choice of action is involved, with further consequences in terms of personal development and self-created destiny or karma.

It is significant also that Truth reaches its third stage during the present Earthly evolutionary phase. Since the 'turning-point of time' the search after Truth—which has resulted in the establishment only of various *truths*—the impetus given to this quest during the past five centuries, and thus coinciding with the Age of the Consciousness Soul, has been enormous. Science has built up a staggering amount of verifiable truths; but it must be said that scientific methodologies depend entirely on what nature is prepared to reveal to it. It seems that, in some curious way, science gives the impression that it 'invents' nature instead of merely succeeding to discover some of its secrets. On the other hand, human ingenuity is providing increasingly sophisticated means for investigation and research, and for more opportunities for science-based technologies to be implemented.

However, it must be said that science as practised at the present time confines itself—and necessarily so—to what is physical and material in the world. It denies the existence of *spirit*, and this, to its great detriment, results in severe limitation in terms of range and scope. Rudolf Steiner bewailed the fact that scientists will never come fully to understand matter until they realize that in matter spirit is perpetually at work. As discussed earlier, the Truth will inevitably remain inaccessible to them until the complementary—and necessary—facts that can be revealed by spiritual science are integrated into the growing corpus of materialist science. We are presently only at the third stage of Truth, but Steiner indicated repeatedly that the time will come when both material and spiritual science will be acknowledged to be necessary for the Truth to be grasped, and this, it is reasonable to suggest, will reach its culmination during the next maturational period of the Earth, namely, the Jupiter evolution. This, it need scarcely be said, is when the Verity of Truth manifests its fourth and final state, and will have been transformed into Wisdom. By then Imagination will have become the appropriate means of perception and conscious experience.

Thus our whole human constitution at this stage will have been subjected, as it were, to increasingly powerful influences of Truth in an archetypal sense since the Old Sun stage of evolution. This was when the etheric principle was added to, or impelled to become active in, our primitive physical-material principle. Now, to put it simply if somewhat crudely, this corporeal organization, having been organized and created by exalted spiritual agencies, being themselves utterly moral, they were obliged to incorporate the factor, element or principle of Truth into that organization. That is to say, our corporeal organization cannot lie, it cannot be representative of anything that is untrue, and the same can of course be said of every other organism *which consists of etheric and physical vehicles only.* Thus, the 'passionless plants' which colonize the lands and waters of the Earth's surface cannot be other than pure in a moral sense.

Needless to say, perhaps, the factor of Justice, then at its second stage, is also influential in all this; it lies at the foundation of all moral and natural law. Rudolf Steiner spoke of Truth, Beauty and Goodness in that order, which is that employed in common speech. However, as we have seen already, this is not a matter of mere chance, for they are so deeply rooted in human nature and culture as to rank as instinctive. The following observations made by him are instructive:

> The world in which we are unconscious in the sleeping state, nor the world in which we are unconscious in the dreaming state—in neither of these worlds does one find goodness ... We can only speak of goodness where there is a distinction between an inner and an outer world, so that goodness can obey the spiritual world or not. In the same way as the state of sleep is assigned to truth and the state of dreaming to beauty, the waking state is assigned to goodness. While awake, therefore, human beings are not disposed in their physical and etheric organisms towards truth, but towards goodness.[16]

With the addition to the human constitution during the Old Moon evolution of our astral nature, temptation and the potential capability to err was inevitably incorporated. It comes as no surprise, therefore, to learn that it is our very astral nature which, during the Jupiter evolution, our ego will be faced with the task of spiritualizing, 'purifying' or ennobling, resulting in the development of spirit-self, and the attainment to Imagination.

Rudolf Steiner associated the members of the Trinity with the Verities as follows: Goodness to God the Father; Beauty to God the Son, and Truth to God the Holy Spirit. It comes as no surprise that he related the three Verities to Time also, declaring that past, present, future as they play their part in human life, assume far-reaching significance when we understand the concrete reality of the other three concepts: Truth, Beauty and Goodness. Furthermore, he related Truth to the physical body, Beauty to the etheric body, and Goodness to the astral body, as we have already discussed. Now when these vehicles have been spiritualized by our ego, we attain to spirit-self, life-spirit and spirit-man respectively, and the fourth stage—and culmination—of each one of the Verities is achieved, again respectively, during the Jupiter, Venus and Vulcan evolutionary periods.

'The truth shall make you free'

As we have seen, Truth is the first of the Verities to have been introduced for development in corresponding fashion to ourselves through the stages of Earthly evolution through time, followed in turn by Beauty and Goodness, and all in accordance with a predetermined pattern. It is only now, during the present Earth evolution, that we have attained to a relatively *conscious* experience of them. It is as though the Divine Powers decreed that there should be a kind of gestatory period for Justice and then each of the Verities in turn. Certainly, four stages are posited, which correspond neatly with the four periods of development of both the Earth and humanity, and this can scarcely be coincidence.

The principal activity associated with everything spiritual is that of *thinking*, and accordingly the spiritual realms harbour thoughts as real beings, perpetually and creatively constructive and actively mobile. In the spiritual worlds thoughts are directly comparable to the elements and compounds of the present mineral world. Steiner's description of archetypes as 'master builders of all that comes into being in the physical and soul worlds' is at once graphic and fitting, particularly in view of the fact that in the spiritual realms thoughts are directly comparable to solid matter of the physical world.

All this being so, we may reasonably assert that there exist in the supersensible worlds archetypes of every phenomenon of a soul or physical-material nature that is to be found in Earthly realms. Obviously, our soul and bodily natures inevitably manifest these spiritual powers. Elsewhere it has been mentioned that our physical body is our oldest and most perfect vehicle, having its origins in the conditions prevailing during the Old Saturn stage of our evolution. The relevant archetypes must therefore have been involved in this, and it necessarily follows that our very bodily constitution represents the manifestation of these to a greater or lesser degree. Furthermore, this process, as appropriate, must have been operative during the succeeding evolutionary stages, when to the physical body provided during the Old Saturn period was added the etheric body (during Old Sun) and the astral body (during Old Moon).

This means that Justice as an archetypal principle was literally incorporated into our nature during the Old Saturn period, thereafter to undergo further development in the succeeding three evolutionary periods, reaching its culmination with the fourth, which is the current Earthly stage. This was not, of course, a process of which we were at all conscious. Rudolf Steiner characterized our existence on Old Saturn to have been that of automatons, when all influences originating in the creative spiritual powers were so to speak 'rayed in' from without. Our consciousness on Old Sun was that of sleep, and we were completely dependent on spiritual agencies for our development, which consisted in the main of the addition of our etheric organization, such as it was at that stage.

Truth was introduced at this stage also as the corresponding archetypal associate of that which found then, and still finds, expression as our etheric nature. Now we know that, just as the etheric as expressed in matter manifests as formative forces operative in our physical-material nature, these same powers are also expressible in complementary fashion as thinking and ideation, memory and other mental functions. Thoughts can be said to exist in the etheric world, and as we have discussed elsewhere, Truth is attainable only through thinking, and as humanity is constituted at the present time this entails the agency of our brain. (This is as far as our present Earthly sense-bound consciousness is concerned. Sense-free thinking is not at issue here.) It is no coincidence, therefore, that our intellectual soul arises by virtue of the ennoblement of our etheric body by our ego, and that our spirit-self will arise by reason of further development.

It is only now, with the birth of our ego at the turning-point of time, that we are able effectively to *realize* the Eternal Verities; in other words *reify* them by bringing them to manifestation in the world. Until now they have been obliged to remain so to speak as undeveloped qualities which have been placed into our nature as human beings stage by stage during Old Saturn, Old Sun and Old Moon, only to be developed to their fullness in due course of time. Rudolf Steiner made this significant observation:

> Science does not attempt to describe human beings in their waking state by ascending from truth through beauty to goodness, but explains everything on the basis of outer, causal necessity, which accords only with the *idea* of truth.[17]

Now before the advent of our present Earth evolution, Truth had already gone through two seminal or gestatory stages, and Beauty one stage—but whilst we lacked consciousness of these happenings. With the birth of our ego we are now able to differentiate between ourselves and the outer world, and are hence in possession of the capability, now in its early stages, of realizing Truth by reason of our increasing facility of arriving at a genuine science, and this by succeeding in confirming the spiritual and material worlds as complementary. In other words, the maya of outer appearance will be acknowledged for what it is, namely, the manifestation of spiritual agencies.

At the same time, with this coinciding ability to achieve consciousness of both inner and outer worlds, we are provided with an arena for the exercising by application of our spiritual, soul and bodily natures through our powers thus granted of thinking, feeling and willing respectively, and these in turn for the purpose of reifying Truth, Beauty and Goodness in the world. By matching all these factors we are rendered capable of attaining Truth by the spiritual power of thinking, of discerning Beauty as against ugliness by exercising our soul-powers of sympathy and antipathy, and effecting acts of Goodness by means of our moral deeds on the physical plane in the interests of our fellows. This means that we human beings are *free* to act in accordance with whatever is True, Beautiful or Good, or not. The choice is entirely ours, and upon it will rest the responsibility for the course our future development towards ultimate perfection will take.

Foundations of Thinking, Feeling and Willing

In thy Thinking World-wide Thoughts are living,
In thy Feeling World-All Forces weaving,
In thy Willing World-Beings working.
Lose thyself in World-wide Thoughts,
Feel thyself through World-All Forces,
Create thyself from Beings of Will.
Yet tarry not in Worlds afar
In dreamy play of thought.
Begin in the vast reaches of the Spirit,
And end in thine own Being's depths.
There thou shalt find eternal aims of Gods,
Knowing thyself in thee.[1]

The origins of Thinking, Feeling and Willing

These three fundamental human faculties, which are expressed in our life of soul, also have their archetypal sources—the beings of the First Hierarchy, the Seraphim, Cherubim and Thrones.[2] Usually called the Spirits of Love, Harmony and Will, their activities are by no means confined to these main attributes. Rudolf Steiner stated that, figuratively speaking, the Thrones have the task of putting into practice the high cosmic thoughts that have been conceived in wisdom, thoughts received by the Seraphim from the Gods (the Trinity) and pondered over by the Cherubim.[3] Correspondences between these and thinking, feeling and willing are abundantly clear. The lofty, wisdom-filled thoughts of the Seraphim are contemplated by the Cherubim, who bring to them the forces of harmony, equilibrium and reason which are associated with feeling in its wider implications, and our faculty of willing mirrors the main function of the Thrones.

Rudolf Steiner contended that the beings of the higher Hierarchies are actually our human ancestors, and that in attempting to characterize the most exalted of these, namely, the First Hierarchy, we can arrive at a good idea of the human being as made in the image of God. These exalted beings are distinguished by the fact that they enjoy the 'immediate gaze of the Godhead', and are 'endowed from the beginning with what human beings must gradually seek over the course of their development', as outlined in the previous chapter. This 'seeking' involves our progressively attaining to ever higher powers of cognition, willing (and by implication feeling) that we shall thereby draw nearer and nearer to the Godhead.[4]

Obviously, whatever our aspirations, aims and endeavours, we have no choice but to start from where we are at the moment, at our present stage of human development. Steiner asserted that each planetary state has a special task, just as each earthly historical epoch has, and that a crucial function of the current Earth evolution is to make it possible for human beings to attain true ego-consciousness by providing the necessary factor of Not Self over against which we are enabled to experience and realize our own Self.[5] Thus the external world of sense functions acts as a foil, thereby enhancing our own individual sense of identity. He also expressed this idea in a meditational verse:

Throughout the wide world there lives and moves
The real Being of Man,
While in the innermost core of Man
The mirror-image of the World is living.

The 'I' unites the two,
And thus fulfils
The meaning of existence.[6]

There is no doubt that we are Heavenly as well as Earthly beings, cosmic as well as terrestrial, and that our relationships with the members of the Spiritual Hierarchies are real and actual, and no distant abstraction or metaphor. Our powers of thinking have close association with the Third Hierarchy, and in this connection it is interesting to reflect that the Archai or Primal Beginnings were undergoing their human stage (not condition) during the Old Saturn evolution. The beings of the Second Hierarchy are related to our life of feeling, which although *experienced* to a great extent by our bodily organism is nonetheless independent of it. Similarly, our brain is the organ of thinking and not its originator or generator. We are not normally conscious of a great many of our bodily processes, which proceed as of themselves; our body is our willing slave, and is frequently simply forgotten about—until disability or disease remind us otherwise. As far as our will is concerned we belong not to our own nature but to that of the exalted First Hierarchy.[7]

We have no option other than to act in certain ways if we are to progress along the appropriate path towards the Godhead, and we have already been equipped to bring this about if we so choose. This means that we are obliged to utilize our divinely endowed powers of Thinking, Feeling and Willing within the constraints of our present circumstances, both Earthly and Heavenly. It must follow from this that the manner in which we implement these three archetypal powers shapes our existence to the extent that our total environment will allow. In this we are obliged to seek the co-operation of our fellow human beings, thus fashioning the bases of national, community and family life, and establishing social structures and organizations as appropriate. These, rather than develop, are *developed*—for they cannot develop without the deployment of will-forces—according to the character of each evolving society in its own particular part of the world, and this by creating its own history within the greater whole.

The archetypal nature of our soul-forces

The three fields of human endeavour are directly expressive of the activity of our life of soul within nature as far as its all-round constraints will permit. Science, Art and Religion reflect human activities within the various cultures world-wide, which are generated and experienced through the expression of individual modes of Thinking, Feeling and Willing respectively. Closely involved in this scenario are the Eternal Verities, which are made manifest by us according to the following table:

Soul force	Eternal Verity	Sphere of activity
Thinking	Truth	Science
Feeling	Beauty	Art
Willing	Goodness	Religion

The archetypal nature of these nine harmoniously inter-related factors is easily recognizable, and their application within particular national and racial communities readily perceptible. The manner in which they were so conferred must also be of interest, and references have been made throughout the text from various points of view, particularly in Chapter 4. There, the 'extra Verity' of Justice is especially featured and discussed. In all considerations concerning our constitution we must be flexible and mobile in our thinking, for the matters involved are complex.

In this context it is interesting to note what Rudolf Steiner had to say in this regard, and much may be gained from it. He characterized 'positive' people as those who, in their experiences of the outer world, are 'capable of retaining at least to some extent the firmness and security of their inner being, and therefore possess clear-cut ideas and conceptions, certain inclinations one way or another, and feelings from which those impressions cannot move them'. By contrast, 'negative' individuals 'easily submit to the changing impressions of life'; they are inclined to be easily influenced by new ideas and notions they meet in others, and to adopt them even to the extent of making them their own by integrating them into their existing body of knowledge. The obvious inference is that considerable benefits accrue if we learn to be positive or negative as circumstances demand, and deliberate in our behaviours.

According to the viewpoint most appropriate to the situation, it may in some circumstances be more expedient to regard our constitution as threefold, comprising spirit, soul and body, and in others as fourfold, comprising physical body, etheric body, astral body and ego (as spiritual principle). Sometimes it is more meaningful to regard our physical and etheric bodies as a single entity, for our 'physical' vehicle is also mineral in constitution, and mineral substances are relatively inert or inanimate unless permeated and organized by the specific life-forces that an etheric 'body' provides. Thus our 'corporeal' nature, our bodily nature proper and complete, comprises both mineral body and life body. Similarly, our 'ego' cannot, in terms of Earthly life at least, function unless it is 'spirit-permeated', for the terms 'spirit' and 'ego' are synonymous in the majority of circumstances. In reality, strict application of such exacting terminology is sheer pedantry, but at the same time the understanding of it must be sound.

Evolution	Verity	Vehicle(s)		Soul faculty	Plane
Old Saturn	(Justice)	Physical		Thinking	Earthly
Old Sun	Truth	Etheric	} Corporeal		
Old Moon	Beauty	Astral		Feeling	Soul
Earth	Goodness	Ego		Willing	Spiritual

This table gives a reasonably good picture of where we stand at present, at the 'turning-point of time' and from where we must move on—to Jupiter, Venus and Vulcan. We are now, with Justice at its fourth and final stage, Truth in its third, Beauty at its second, and Goodness at its first stage, well placed for this (discussed in the following chapter). It is also interesting in that it shows clearly the interrelationships among the factors involved, and the patterns that are discernible offer much of value for meditative work.

The reciprocal values of Truth and Goodness were discussed in the previous chapter in order to show how it is that Beauty consistently maintains its central position. The enormous importance of spiritualizing our thinking, and of striving for Truth by way of Beauty and Goodness, is plain to see. Moreover, after death, when our corporeal vehicles have been cast aside, the principles of Justice and Truth/Goodness are applied to good effect during kamaloka (the period immediately after death when we experience our former Earthly life in reverse order as a great tableau), as is Beauty during our passage through the soul world, and Goodness/ Truth during our passage through the spiritual world proper.

Realizing our soul-faculties

Our soul members are, strictly speaking, transitional in nature; that is to say, they are essentially temporary, emanating as they do from fields of interaction between our spirit members and our corporeal members. We are able to establish that the 'soul' arises from the interaction between the eternal spirit on the one hand and the temporary vehicle, the physical body, on the other. In its function as mediator between spirit and body, it is supremely placed for allowing our spiritual nature to experience the outer material world in the shape of our reactions to it, and the lessons learned from it. Our spiritual principle is unable to experience matter directly; the soul, which has its existence between the two polar opposites, takes up what we undergo by virtue of our corporeal principles and passes on the harvest of experience to our higher self or spirit. When the body which it occupies dies, then it too must perish; for it is only the spirit that is truly immortal.

Imprudent talk of an 'immortal soul' can be misleading, inasmuch as it is astral in essence rather than purely spiritual. After the soul has passed through the seven regions of the soul world after death, and released the spirit into the spiritual realms proper, it dissolves into the 'starry' reaches of universal astrality. However, a 'soul-seed' or 'extract' is preserved, to be implanted as a kind of monad[8] into our astral nature by the appropriate spiritual hierarchies in the period preceding our next incarnation, as a kind of nucleus around which the 'new' soul will be organized by the taking up of universal astral substance as appropriate. There exists much confusion in this area, for in this process the factor of continuity is undoubtedly engaged. From this point of view it can be claimed that the soul does possess attributes of immortality, and hence may, from certain points of view, be deemed to be immortal. Involved in all this is our spirit-filled ego, and by the very premise that spirit is by nature indestructible we are, whether we like it or not, whether we believe it or not, unquestionably *immortal*.

However, it is of the greatest importance that we *experience* this immortality, and this is another area of paramount significance which may not perhaps be easy to grasp, but which should nevertheless be clearly understood.[9] A simple table will make matters clear:

Reincarnating	Spirit	Imperishable
Temporarily arising	Soul	Passing away (after death)
Hereditary	Body	Perishable

The soul lives in the fields of tension or interaction set up by the opposing qualities of our spirit-filled ego and our bodily or corporeal nature, which comprises the physical vehicle with its supporting etheric organization. Moreover, we know that the forces of sympathy and antipathy reside in our feeling, which when confronting our spiritual nature in antipathetic fashion gives rise to our thinking; and when in sympathetic fashion it affects our corporeal nature, the impulse for action arises. To put matters somewhat crudely, sympathy and antipathy are represented by the forces of attraction and repulsion, or love and hate, liking and disliking; but it is important to remember that these two sets of factors are in polar opposition, and if equilibrium is not reasonably well maintained all kinds of difficulties present themselves. The balancing out of these two forces is achieved by the application of our powers of *reasoning*, and in this the ego is necessarily involved.[10]

Our *thinking* faculty is spiritual in terms of human nature, and thought is universal, in that concepts employed in one language are translatable into others. Put another way, thinking is a spiritual activity, one which enables us to create our own ideas, and grasp with our powers of understanding the concerns of others. Thoughts are indeed realities, and our ideals with their aims, goals and objectives enable us to marshal all our mental powers. These are employed in observation, research, analysis, seeking causes and reasons, promoting argument and counter-argument, and so on. It is only by thinking that we are able to apprehend what is truthful in the world, and by which we can grasp and assimilate its built-in wisdom. We may talk about 'having a feeling for truth', and indeed there is a sound basis for this inexactness which cannot be proved by resorting to logic or deductive reasoning. This 'thinking with the heart' engages our feeling life, which occupies a position midway between that of thinking on the one hand and willing on the other. It is partly permeated by our conscious awareness that is characteristic of thinking, and partly by willing, which always bears within it attributes of unconsciousness. In other words, it is representative of a dream consciousness over against both our waking consciousness and our consciousness in sleep. Rudolf Steiner had this to say:

> The objective content of a judgement remains firmly fixed outside the realm of feeling, but in order that the subjective human soul may become *convinced* of the rightness of the judgement, feeling must be aroused. When you trace the element of feeling on the one hand in cognition, in thinking, and on the other hand by willing, then you will say: feeling stands as a soul activity midway between cognition and willing, and radiates its nature out in both directions. Feeling is cognition which has not yet

come fully into being, and it is also will which has not yet fully come into being; it is cognition in reserve, and willing in reserve.[11]

We know from common experience that thinking and feeling are frequently so intermixed that one transmutes into the other. We have to have the wish or feeling based either on emotion or expediency to think, ponder and reflect. But we also know that it is easier to find feelings for our reasons than reasons for our feelings, for it is easier to accomplish detached thinking than detached feeling. So in a certain sense we must have to *love* what we choose to think about before we feel actually impelled to embark on formulating thoughts and ideas. Very often this love can develop into devotion, and 'to be devoted to the task', whatever it is, is often a powerful incentive not only to thinking what is necessary but for doing it as well. Emotional commitment is a vital ingredient, as it acts as a stimulus for action. Generally speaking, if we don't want to think about anything we feel is unpleasant or distasteful we try to put the matter out of our minds altogether, however temporarily.

Psychologists, educationists and others would do well to study the implications of Rudolf Steiner's observation that feeling is thinking in reserve, and also willing in reserve. The life of the soul exists in the expression of our thinking, feeling and willing as inner stimuli for outer conduct. Equidistant between the two behavioural poles of willing and thinking lies feeling, which is truly representative of our soul-life. From its central position between thinking and willing, feeling is of course nicely placed to be influenced by, and in turn to influence, both of these opposite soul-qualities and thus our faculties of sympathy and antipathy which are in ceaseless oscillation during our waking hours. The human heart (feeling) acts as balancing agent between our head (thinking) and our metabolic/limbs system (willing). This is a typical indication of how the whole world is a result of the working of countless manifestations of the working of balance.[12]

Most people realize that knowledge acquired by reason of our hearts can be just as important, if not as exact, as that acquired through our heads. Moreover, our faculty of feeling is often called in to inspire us to action, so that our ideals—and those of others, perhaps—may be fulfilled and realized. Our feelings and emotions sway back and forth, our likes and dislikes wax and wane, our joys and woes come and go; and such experiences seem to be more immediate, and closer to us than our thoughts, which usually take on a more distant character than our feelings. We are of course speaking of the general area of the *soul*, the bearer of all our sympathies and antipathies, and arguably the primary agent of incentive for action. Our inner lives are for the most part dominated by our life of soul, for if we don't *feel* attracted by a certain idea it is often dismissed from our minds; it is usually unhappy people who carry out actions they do not feel like doing. Such motivation is *intrinsic* in character, whereas *extrinsic* motivation has rather to do with outer demands—the kinds that have to be met whether we like it or not.

The whole business of action is that of the will, and deeds necessarily involve the limbs, the employment of the strength and capabilities of the body. Obviously, the mere action of thinking, which is confined to our head, cannot of its own power get things done in the outer world—and the same can be said of our feelings. Both faculties have to be expressed or implemented by means of our limbs and in many cases their extension in the shape of tools and mechanical aids of various sorts. This is how the human spirit, which is totally powerless on the physical plane, achieves its aims and intentions, and brings about changes in the outside world. Obviously, the results or consequences of such actions and events which have been brought about by human agency is subject to appraisal and other kinds of 'feedback', so that the spirit may in turn inspire and motivate further action of whatever kind. These notions are also easily made plain:

Principle	Verity	Soul Faculty	Manifestation
Spirit	Truth	Thinking	Ideas
Soul	Beauty	Feeling	Incentives
Body	Goodness	Willing	Deeds

The special nature of the will

From many points of view it may be said the whole human being is primarily one of will, and Steiner made this plain.[13] He was fully aware of the difficulties attendant upon securing a firm grasp of what the will actually is. Today, as in his own time, most psychologists regard it as a barely differentiated mass of conative elements somehow appended to our faculties of thinking and/or feeling. Just as thinking is a 'waking' activity and feeling a 'dreaming' activity, willing is best characterized as a 'sleeping' activity because it is largely an unconscious process: any act of will is not truly effected or realized as such until it has been done. Any deed we perform must entail our limbs, our bodily organization, the genesis of which is traceable to the exalted Spirits of Will or Thrones, at the Old Saturn stage of evolution, and the correlationships are not difficult to discern. They poured themselves out in order to grant us existence, and now, at the Earth stage of development, matter is the most solid—and indeed resistant—form of these will-forces. The task facing us in the future is the spiritualization in turn of our astral, etheric and physical-material vehicles. As mentioned earlier, at present our spiritual members, namely, spirit-self, life-spirit and spirit-man, exist in seminal form only.

As we are constantly thrusting ourselves as it were into the future, it can easily be seen why Steiner always stressed the seedlike nature of our will, which is the bearer of potential for the future. In the following table we find *motive* (which is undeniably a factor that is ego-driven) in the central position, when the ego begins to operate on the Earthly plane—a fact of great significance. We can readily see that the model of the human being in its sevenfold pattern as set out earlier can be applied to the development of our will-nature also, with which the considerable powers of the ego are so closely allied:

Earth evolution	Human Principle	Will-element
Old Saturn	Physical body	Instinct
Old Sun	Etheric body	Impulse
Old Moon	Astral body	Desire
Earth	Ego, as soul kernel	Motive
Jupiter	Spirit-self as transmuted astral body	Wish
Venus	Life-spirit as transmuted etheric body	Intention
Vulcan	Spirit-man as transmuted physical body	Resolution

The forces of instinct, impulse and desire, which we share with the animal world, were bestowed in cumulative fashion during Old Saturn, Old Sun and Old Moon respectively. However, we human beings were so to speak *individualized* during the late stage of the Lemurian Age, since which time the powers of our ego have gradually developed. It can readily be seen from this table how it comes about that when the ego, in its work of ennobling and purifying the astral body/sentient soul with its characteristics of what might be termed 'raw' *desire* with which we were endowed on Old Moon, the more refined and conscious agency of *wish* will—ideally, of course—be engendered on Jupiter. Similarly, the primitive *impulses* with which we were bestowed on Old Sun, and firmly based in our etheric body and manifesting as temperament-based drives, are transmuted into consciously arrived at *intentions* on Venus. Finally, on Vulcan the *instinctual* urges rooted in our bodily nature, which were gifted to us on Old Saturn, are due—if all has gone well for us—to be transformed into firmest *resolution*. These processes relate in detail with the table in Chapter 2 which maps our ever-growing powers at the appropriate levels of consciousness.

Now, at the present stage of evolution, we experience the remaining three factors, namely, wish (earnest rather than frivolous), intention (serious) and resolution (unyielding) as mere representations of the dominant forces they will become. They reside in seedlike form in our spirit-self, life-spirit and spirit-man respectively, and will not normally operate to maximal effectiveness until, as a result of exerting the powers of our ego progressively throughout the Jupiter, Venus and Vulcan evolutionary periods, these three members will have evolved by dint of regular maturational processes.

We are thus equipped, by reason of our acquisition of enhanced powers by our ego, to exercise choice, and increasingly able to wield our powers of freedom. Rudolf Steiner often referred to humanity as the Hierarchy of Love and Freedom, and his philosophy of *ethical individualism* can be seen to be entirely appropriate to the current Age of the Consciousness Soul. With reference to this, he gave stern warning that love without freedom is essentially meaningless, and that freedom without love is destructive. Biblical scriptures exhort us to love God with all our heart, all our soul and all our might (Deuteronomy 6:5f), and Rudolf Steiner confirmed that the higher hierarchies are indeed gratified to receive human love offered up in freedom.

We know that the divine Father-principle is represented in the cosmos as material nature, that His essential Being is that of Goodness, and that Goodness epitomizes the purest morality. Furthermore, the ego, as soul-kernel, operates not only through our astral body but also through the forces of the sentient, intellectual and consciousness soul members which arise as a result of its ennobling influences. The laws of the spiritual world are moral laws, and so a definite pattern begins to emerge. Goodness has its being and manifestation in our deeds—deeds of goodness, morality and virtue—and in performing them we are expressing our *will;* and this is why in carrying out works of goodness we are at the same time acting in accordance with the will of God. It is this kind of thinking that lies behind the saying of Angelus Silesius: 'Is my will dead, God must do what I will; I myself prescribe to him the pattern and the goal.' His will was of course far from being 'dead'—it was actively seeking to do God's will.

Moreover, we know that purely intellectual methods of teaching and learning run counter to the needs of humanity as a whole, and Steiner stressed that we should realize that the acquisition of knowledge should be in the service of the gods. Selfish manipulation of knowledge, he warned, runs counter to true human progress. An echo of this instinctive knowledge can be found in the work of those who strove actively to express the Beautiful, earnestly sought for Truth, or faithfully performed the appropriate deeds to express Goodness, for right up until the late nineteenth century this ideal was reflected in the custom of anonymously dedicating all work accomplished to the greater glory of God: *Ad majorem Dei gloriam.* This noble ideal was their incentive for doing so in realization of their purpose: to serve the Divine Powers as best they knew. Rudolf Steiner himself declared:

> Be clear that the acquisition of knowledge must be in the service of the gods. Ahriman is able to do something with knowledge that is not acquired in the service of the gods. This knowledge is taken over into the service of Ahriman, and establishes his power.[14]

Thus it truly comes about that matters are indeed arranged to the pattern 'As above, so below; as below, so above', and that God's will really is done on Earth as it is in Heaven. The archetypal Verities of Goodness, Beauty and Truth, made manifest by the human soul-forces of Willing, Feeling and Thinking, ensure that this be so.

The 'Three Merits': Wonder, Compassion and Conscience

As we know, the Christ Impulse as such was present on the Earth for three years, and during this time was incarnated into, and made use of the physical, etheric and astral bodies of Jesus of Nazareth, for it had none of Its own. Furthermore, we know that the Christ Being will remain united with the earth 'even to the end of the Age'. The Christ Impulse endures and will be received into humanity during the course of Earth evolution—but how? Rudolf Steiner asserted that whatever manifests as Wonder, Compassion and Conscience that has lived in human beings since the Christ Event, and continues so to live, serves to provide respectively the astral, etheric and 'physical' body of the Christ Impulse Itself.[15] He further affirmed that this establishes the true meaning of the passage in Matthew 25:40 with regard to those who will qualify to 'inherit the kingdom provided for you from the foundation of the world'. In all our dealings in society we should bear in mind Christ's words of admonishment: 'Inasmuch as ye have done [it] unto one of the least of these my brethren, ye have done it to me.'

Rudolf Steiner spoke about these matters with great earnestness, and what he had to say echoes Paul's words to the letter, and is worth quoting in full:

> Whatever wrongs are committed in these three realms [wonder, compassion, conscience] deprive the Christ of the full possibility of full development on the Earth; that is to say, Earth evolution is left imperfect. Those who go about the Earth with indifference and unconcern, who have no urge to understand what the earth can reveal to them, deprive the astral body of Christ of the possibility of full development; those who live without unfolding compassion and love hinder the etheric body of Christ from full development, and those who lack conscience impede the development of what corresponds to the physical body of Christ ... but this means that the Earth cannot reach the goal of its evolution.[16]

We are therefore called upon to acknowledge the connections between our own three sheaths, the three Eternal Verities, the three soul-forces, and the three great Merits, and to make them manifest during our Earthly lives by living into them by all the power we can muster. These relationships can be seen at a glance:

Merit	Soul-force	Verity	Vehicle
Wonder	Thinking	Truth	Astral body
Compassion	Feeling	Beauty	Etheric body
Conscience	Willing	Goodness	Physical body

The correlations among these factors are discussed from many viewpoints in other parts of this book, and their importance in terms of the principles by which we live our daily lives cannot be overrated or overestimated. They are truly archetypal in nature and expression, and what is enacted by each individual is necessarily manifested within society as a whole, and indeed the world itself, for good or ill. This notion of the 'body social' is directly analogous to that of the apostle Paul in I Corinthians, Chapter 12, where he compares it—ideally, of course—to 'the body of Christ' as its manifestation and extension in the world. However, such matters are profound, and their realization and acknowledgement is very limited.

We have now reached the situation where we simply take freedom of choice for granted. Long gone are the millennia when we were under the aegis of the gods, under whom there was no such thing as free will. With regard to the Christ Being, however, there is simply no compulsion,[17] and it is rather a matter of making our own choices and taking the consequences in terms of our individual destiny and every other aspect of our progress towards perfection. Conversely, compulsion is the weapon of the Antichrist.[18] It is of the greatest importance for the furtherance of proper development of both ourselves and the Earth itself that the principle of egotism, which is now becoming increasingly widespread, be overcome. By the exercising of Wonder, Compassion and Conscience we shall render it more and more possible to ensure that the Earth reaches its goal in evolutionary terms.

However, as we have seen, we must learn to acknowledge certain truths about moral standards, fellow-feeling, the energetic cultivation of factors such as conscience, and to work harmoniously with the influences proceeding from the primordial archetypes that we have been considering. In respect of these we have to make our own decisions involving the Christ Impulse, in full realization of the consequences for ourselves as individuals, Humankind at large, and the very Earth itself. Our several responsibilities are indeed great, and we have a moral duty to make these known and under-stood—and moreover, implemented. In this respect the Lord's Prayer is potentially an enormously powerful incentive. If we fail in these respects we endanger the opportu-nities for evolution itself to proceed.[19]

Deploying our soul-forces

Rudolf Steiner indicated on many occasions that Religion, Art and Science, as representative of Goodness, Beauty and Truth respectively, were originally a unity, and thus by implication consist of common stuff. He also, in terms of the Trinity, assigned Goodness to God the Father, Beauty to the Son, and Truth to the Holy Spirit. Without going into such niceties as whether Son and Holy Spirit 'proceeded from' the Father, or are integral to the Father in some way, it seems reasonably clear that the pre-eminent source or first principle is indeed God the Father, who alone is, and to be called, *good* (Matthew 19:17). As everything proceeds from the Godhead, it can be safely inferred that whatever is beautiful and true also proceeds from Goodness, morality; the element of synonymity is undoubtedly present. Wherever all these characteristics—uprightness, righteousness and purity—are made manifest, Justice is seen to be present also.

It is impossible to discuss the three Verities without relating them to our three soul-forces of thinking, feeling and willing, and also to what I have, in deference to Rudolf Steiner, called the 'Three Merits' of Wonder, Compassion and Conscience, as mentioned earlier on. These three attri-butes are inevitably part of our experiences of a soul-nature during our sojourn on the Earthly plane, and which figure large in our 'education' process. He pointed out that the propensity we have for wondering about our own nature as well as that of the universe, our innate urge to understand, or at least make sense of our environment, forms the basis of all philosophical thinking in its broadest sense. It is noteworthy that natural philosophy was taught in universities long before it became natural science, which in turn was broken down into the various disciplines of physics, chemistry, biology and so on that we know today.

Compassion or fellow-feeling, the kind of unconditional, brotherly or Christian love best represented by the Greek word *agape*, obviously belongs to the realm of feeling, but also to that of willing. The Good Samaritan not only felt pity for the traveller who fell among thieves, but he also did something about it. Concerning compassion, Rudolf Steiner gave this verse upon which to ponder often:

So long as you feel the pain
Which I am spared,
The Christ unrecognized
Is working in the world.
For weak still is the spirit
Whilst each is capable of suffering
Only through their own body.[20]

It is by dint of compassion that we are able to experience not only sympathy but also empathy with our fellows; not only feeling for them but feeling with them, placing ourselves as it were into their world, and stepping into their shoes. In short, if we are incapable of active charity we are morally defective. The third essentially human quality we should cultivate is that of conscience, that certain point of reference which we experience in the depths of our being by which we are able to appraise a given situation and make moral judgements concerning it and, ideally at any rate, acting accordingly. By curbing our self-interest and adopting as far as possible a detached, objective viewpoint we become less selfish and more altruistic. Ideally, the stirrings of our conscience should prompt us to correct our tendencies towards unprincipled impulses and any temptation to behave in a self-indulgent manner. In this regard Steiner had this observation to make:

> ... sharpness of conscience [should be] the prerequisite of any spiritual movement. If we lack this sharpness of conscience, if we do not feel the most intense responsibility to the holiest truth, we shall make no progress on any other path ... it will above all be necessary to have eyes for the quality of love and compassion.[21]

Another threefold relationship with our faculties of Thinking, Feeling and Willing, seen to be supportive indirectly of Truth and Beauty, and directly of Goodness, is expressed as Faith, Hope and Love (Charity), all respectively, which represent the three so-called Theological Virtues. Goodness, as love in action, is singled out by the apostle Paul in his well-known eulogy to love in I Corinthians 13, as the greatest of the three. He places love, in the sense of *agape*, above every other human virtue or attribute, for it 'all things covers' (*panta stegei*), and when it is considered that universal love is the primary characteristic of God Himself, there can be little argument. Love 'endures' and 'never fails', 'rejoices in the truth', 'believes all things' and 'hopes all things', and by thus 'covering' all things of whatever nature or substance emerges as the supreme Virtue, descriptive as it is of the Supreme Deity. Paul sums up his discourse: 'And now (*nuni de*—at this time) abide faith (*pistis*—[religious] faith, belief, trust); hope (*elpis* [Christian] hope in the sense rather of unfeigned expectation), and (unconditional) love (*agape*—love, good will) and the greatest of these is love.'

It is reasonable to contend that the three Eternal Verities as we know them today are not only seen to engage our three soul-forces but also are identifiable with Faith, Hope and Love. Obviously, Love reigns supreme, inasmuch as it is effectively synonymous with God's peerless attribute of Goodness. In the same letter Paul states that knowledge (*gnosis*) 'shall be done away' also, but Love 'rejoices in' the Truth, and 'believes' or has trust or confidence in all things, and this with 'hope'. This must be so, for the element of Hope is closely related to confidence in the future, and this in the sense of admitting to a certain powerlessness, and perhaps even helplessness, regarding future events, as our being ultimately reliant on the all-wise Godhead, relying on 'the ever-present help of the spiritual world'.

Rudolf Steiner asserted that faith in its occult sense means that one must never allow one's judgement of the future to be influenced by the past, and the future must be faced with new faith 'in all things'. This attitude, put rather crudely, can be construed as 'faith in the universe'. As an initiate himself, Paul could say this with conviction. In the time of Paul there existed nothing that could be called 'science' in the modern sense, and little in the philosophical sense of deliberately seeking to unravel the secrets of nature. Wisdom was the overall term employed for what was known to be true in the knowledge of Heavenly and Earthly things as it affected humanity.

Steiner confirmed that what the pupils of the Mystery Centres perceived as wisdom was at the same time art and beauty, and that 'the yearning for truth and beauty, wisdom and art, as well as religious impulses developed simultaneously: science, art and religion were one.'[22] Matters relating to these three areas were not *described*, but brought to the pupils in living pictures, and not by appealing to the intellect, reason, logic and so on. Now, more than two millennia later, it is an important part of the task of spiritual science to reunify these three areas of human striving, and grant them each and severally the proper importance owed to them as truly representational of their archetypal inspirers: Truth, Beauty and Goodness.

Steiner Education as a Demand of the Age

To wonder at beauty,
To stand guard over truth,
To look up to the noble,
To decide for the good,
Leads us on our journey
To goals for our life,
To right in our doing,
To peace in our feeling,
To light in our thinking;
And teaches us trust
In the guidance of God
In all that there is
In the wide World-All,
In the soul's deep soil.[1]

Parents and teachers have a sacred task

As has been maintained throughout, we are primarily spiritual beings, and only secondarily physical-material beings. We have each been guided in our 'descent' from the world of spirit into the world of matter by exalted spiritual beings, and the fact that our children have been in a certain sense 'given' to us may well invoke feelings of awe and wonder—at least until they are old enough to 'play up' and make life appear somewhat less miraculous and more quotidian.

Parents are deeply involved in the education process as well as teachers. Whether they realize it or not, together they inevitably and consistently bring the children in their charge into direct involvement with the actualities of the Eternal Verities, the archetypes of Goodness, Beauty and Truth that are built into the whole of nature and the entire human constitution. In effect they are charged with a sacred trust; there are no other words to describe it.

The child is faced with a difficult and complex task, namely, that of a spiritual being having to integrate itself with the material body provided by its parents according to the laws of heredity. For this to come about successfully, the fullest possible co-operation is required on the part of parents and significant others to effect the determining rudimentary processes of socialization, and later teachers and helpers for that of education. Rudolf Steiner emphasized that this process of integration cannot come about of itself; the co-operation of parents and teachers is needed, and if this is not forthcoming the whole operation may well fail. These are weighty words, but Steiner was never more earnest in his exhortations to parents and teachers alike to shoulder this intimidating but enormously important and significant task. In his own words:

> If you take up educational work knowing that what affects the young child will continue through the whole of its life as happiness or unhappiness, sickness or health, then at first this knowledge may seem a burden to your souls; but it will also spur you on to develop forces and capacities, and above all an attitude of mind as a teacher strong enough to sow 'seeds of the soul' in the young child which will only blossom later in life, perhaps in old age. This is the knowledge of man which anthroposophy sets forth as the basis of the art of education.[2]

However, mainstream educationists are forced to admit that the very thing they need most is entirely lacking, and that is a genuine philosophy of education: a sound and viable pedagogy, curriculum and didactics; an education which retains the childlike enthusiasm for lifelong learning. The very inconsistencies and endless stream of 'reforms' in the orthodox educational sector show that this is not the case. Steiner or Waldorf education, formulated by Rudolf Steiner out of a thorough knowledge of the true nature of the human being and the demands of the present age, is grounded on a sound rationale, and can, by reason of its universal character, be implemented by every culture on the surface of the globe. Concerning this, he said:

> Of necessity our educational task will differ from the educational tasks which mankind has set itself hitherto. Not that we are so vain and proud as to imagine that we, of ourselves, should initiate a new world-wide order in education, but because from anthroposophical spiritual science we know that the epochs of evolution as they succeed each other must always set humanity fresh tasks.[3]

Steiner's educational principles are consistent, and their validity can be confirmed by observation and the application of rigorous scientific standards. This art of education has stood the test of time, having been introduced in 1919 by Steiner when the first Waldorf School was founded in Stuttgart. Since then the number of schools in more than 50 countries which have adopted his educational ideas number well over 700 (in 1999). Contrary to what is sometimes stated, Waldorf education has not become somehow 'out of date', because it is being constantly renewed by the teachers who implement the fundamental principles involved, and it allows for cultural variations and appropriateness of curriculum. Moreover, the archetypal forces upholding the philosophy and practice of such an art of education can never be out of date, for they have been there as needed in the past and will be operative as appropriate in the future also.

The importance of proper socialization and education

Nowadays, a significant proportion of the socializing process lies with child-minders, helpers and carers, and all too often this is very much a haphazard undertaking, with over-reliance on instinctual drives and traditional customs. Parents and teachers—indeed everyone who has contact with children—can, in the last resort, do no other than 'teach themselves', inevitably transmitting their own moral and other standards, a fact that is all too often overlooked in terms of responsibility and accountability. As a general principle it can be contended that the Eternal Verities cannot be taught, but have to be 'lived with', 'lived into' or somehow experienced in our inner nature; that is to say, there should be nurturing of the children's soul-faculties as well as direct instruction. Naturally, we learn from the feelings aroused in us, for these in turn affect our thoughts and our actions, and prompt further reactions and responses in an endless chain of events.

Goodness is associated with our bodily nature and willing, Beauty with our etheric nature and feeling, and Truth with our astral nature and thinking, and it is the orchestrating of these that should form the very basis of all education. It bears repetition that the contents of the curriculum should be so formulated and presented to the pupils as to bring this about by the implementation of appropriate teaching strategies. The curriculum should be so arranged as to demonstrate in every possible manner the multitudinous relationships between humankind and the world we all share. That is to say, all education should take its start from the nature of the human being—there is no other way.

It is perhaps not sufficiently widely known that it is through our soul-faculties that we involve the corresponding principles of Truth, Beauty and Goodness not only in our daily lives but also, by reason of this, in our life after death.[4] We know, for example, that anything in the manner of untruth, lies or deceit cannot be tolerated in the spiritual world, where moral laws obtain. Consequently, during our passage through the soul world that which we bear within us of an immoral nature is subject to purifying influences. We should heed the exhortations of Paul in his letter to the Philippians (4:8) and ponder well whatsoever things are true, venerable, just, pure, lovely and of good report, praiseworthy and virtuous.

It goes without saying that Rudolf Steiner did all he could

to encourage everyone, especially teachers, to maintain high moral standards. He reminded them never to make bargains with anything untruthful, to 'have courage for the truth'[5] at all times. Similarly, he exhorted parents of very young children not to harbour untruthful, ugly or impure thoughts, and to cultivate the beautiful in art and in nature alike. He advised parents and teachers to exhibit antipathy, in the form of disgust and revulsion, as hating the bad and the obnoxious, and showing sympathy by embracing the good and the lovely wherever these might be found, and to adopt creatively artistic mèthods of teaching. Goodness should remain as a fundamental mood of the soul. He advised the religion teachers of the first Waldorf School to foster the kind of religious feelings in the pupils as they themselves were able to gain from their own anthroposophical world-outlook, to convey the notion that we are all made in the image of God, and that it is our duty to be good.

The urge to express feelings of gratitude to the Powers who are greater than ourselves is deeply rooted in tradition, as evidenced by the many and diverse kinds of thanksgiving, both formal and informal. This is entirely appropriate, especially during the stage of early childhood, as well as the habit of giving and sharing, which should be encouraged. Who has not been offered remnants of a sticky bun or a sodden, half-eaten biscuit by a generous, well-meaning toddler? Love is freely given as well as received during the whole of childhood, and ideally the range of the lower school pupils' experience should widen and deepen to embrace their immediate community, and eventually the entire world.

Orthodox educationists and teachers are inclined to adopt a far too simplistic view of the children they seek to serve. In all sincerity they relate the whole educational process as one of stimulus and response, input and output; that is to say, pupils are expected to pour out what has been previously poured in, on the traditional 'regurgitation' model. The National Curriculum (in Great Britain), with its crude processes of examination and testing, the setting up of abstract targets, determining levels of achievement and so on, was set up on this very basis, which closely resembles the 'production-line' procedures seen to be at work in all organizations committed to the realm of economics. This kind of thing was abhorred by Rudolf Steiner, who firmly held that responsible teachers should be left free to use their own professional judgement as circumstances demand. In a lecture to the prospective teachers of the first Waldorf school he declared that 'a system of teaching which lays down beforehand the teacher's timetable and every imaginable limitation actually, and moreover completely, excludes the teacher's art'.

It is not without significance that the government department concerned with all this is called the Department of Education *and Employment*, for the ideal of utilitarianism reigns supreme, and the popular but fallacious notion that the main purpose and aim of education is 'to get a job' and 'to get on in life' is accorded strong governmental support, and children are being blatantly and constantly indoctrinated into this in attitude and belief.

Modern society is finding it extremely difficult to adjust to the enormously rapid rates of change now taking place. These require degrees of versatility, flexibility and adaptability in the population which are all too rarely forthcoming. There has long been much debate about just how to set about educating 'the whole person', but this cannot and will not be achieved without a genuine recognition and acceptance of the fact by educational authorities that human beings are primarily spiritual in nature, and not little animals that have somehow to be 'humanized'. However, orthodox educational methodologies amount to little more than training along certain well-defined lines laid down by centralized authority. All kinds of 'rewards' in the way of stars, certificates, prizes and suchlike are awarded to winners in the course of such training, whilst the under-achievers, poor performers and losers are discreetly sidelined.

We must be fully conscious of exactly how children are affected, directly and indirectly, by orthodox educational practices now being implemented, thoroughly inappropriate as they are to modern times and conditions. Rudolf Steiner warned of trouble ahead as far back as 1919, when he stated that unless anthroposophical spiritual knowledge was brought into the domain of pedagogy and didactics, police would be needed to keep order in schools.[6] As we all know, this is the case today in many educational establishments, but nowadays hospitals, shopping malls, supermarkets and other public places all have variously appropriate security arrangements, from patrolling guards to coded doorlocks and closed-circuit television monitoring devices. His words are more true today than they were in 1919, when he said:

> As you think about it, just notice how many cruelties permeate our culture, cruelties with which the cruelties of barbarian times cannot be compared ... Two examples in evidence of this can definitely be seen today: people who are very intelligent and who have a decided inclination toward evil; and many others who subconsciously suppress but do not fight this inclination toward evil, merely letting their intelligence sleep. Drowsiness of the soul; or, with wakeful souls, a strong inclination toward evil and error—this may be observed at present.[7]

Matters have got steadily worse during the years since Steiner uttered these words despite 'enrichment programmes', 'compensatory learning' and other such remedial schemes. Current orthodox educational methodologies being inflicted upon children below the age of puberty are outworn, outdated and inappropriate. The results of what I have called 'pedagogical vandalism' in the final chapter of my book *Steiner Education in Theory and Practice* are now increasingly to be seen in the majority of schools in many countries. The young instinctively know that they are in a very real sense being abused, and are rebelling—by vandalizing, truanting, under-achieving, giving verbal and physical harassment to parents, fellow-pupils, teachers and the general public. This behaviour is expressive of their overall resistance to being coerced into ways of learning *which do not meet their needs.*

Parallel stages in world and human evolution

Rudolf Steiner declared that one of the most important features of Waldorf education is that the curriculum should be regarded not so much as a body of knowledge to be transmitted to the pupils, but rather as a vehicle for the conscious exercising of their faculties of thinking, feeling and willing. This in turn achieves a certain balance between the powers of cognition (acquisition of knowledge), affect (arousal of the feelings), and conation (the urge to purposeful action). By doing this, teachers exercise the children's powers of spirit, soul and body respectively, by bringing truly holistic philosophies and methodologies to their whole pedagogy, and establishing harmony and balance among these three principles and their application in terms of socialization and education. Steiner contended that our three soul-powers will gradually become less and less integrated, and that a thorough knowledge of the complicated nature of the human being will be required in order for individuals to 'hold themselves together'.[8]

It seems patently absurd, in times of accelerating accumulation of knowledge and instant access to it by modern techniques of information technology, that so much emphasis is placed in mainstream educational practices for children, and even infants, on learning whatever is deemed to be 'useful', and moreover be tested on it—and this when the accepted wisdom of today is tomorrow's fallacy. For the most part, the orthodox learning process appeals almost exclusively to the pupils' cognitive skills, and is therefore one-sided. It seems not to occur to conventional educationists that the formative years of childhood is the proper time for exercising skills that their charges, as pupils, students and adults, will be practising at every waking moment for the rest of their lives—that is to say, *their faculties of thinking, feeling and willing*. If they understood this they would understand why Steiner insisted that education should address the question 'What should a person be?' rather than

'What should a person know?' Needless to say, he included teachers in this, going as far as warning prospective teachers of the first Waldorf School: 'You can only become good teachers and educators if you pay attention not merely to what you *do*, but what you *are*.'[9]

Spiritual science ably demonstrates that the education and socialization of children into their particular community and culture comprises three distinct stages. The first extends through infancy, when spirit, soul and body are an integrated—and to a great extent an undifferentiated—whole, and when that which influences one principle necessarily influences the other two. It is during this stage that the powers of willing become established, and continue to develop. And this is when the powers of imitation are at their strongest, and the bodily constitution of the child is largely determined, for what is imitated is imprinted into its whole organism—particularly the brain and nervous system. It is at this time, therefore, that Goodness is the proper Verity to be inculcated, when an attitude of religious devotion may be said actually to exude from the infant, radiating in all directions, making demands on its parents and carers which it cannot yet articulate, for them to reciprocate.

Nowadays, psychologists and others regard the traditional classification of the life of the soul into thinking, feeling and willing as being too loose as well as unscientific. However, it is possible to demonstrate that there are very sound reasons from the point of view of the evolution of our planet as well as ourselves as to why we are organized in the manner we are. The foundations of our present physical body were laid during the Old Saturn evolution, but it consisted only of heat, and this was differentiated only in the most primitive of ways.[10] This was the first stage of our evolution, and when Justice as an archetypal feature first manifested itself. Pure morality reigned supreme, and the principle of Justice, then in its first phase, prevailed unchallenged. In addition, the rudiments of what is now our superbly designed and developed physical body, which is such a willing servant to our ego with its will-impulses, were laid down.

However, it must be borne in mind that we were completely oblivious of what was going on, as we were utterly under the control and direction of beings of the higher hierarchies, and our consciousness was that of deep sleep. This stage is paralleled with the first seven-year developmental period in a child's life, when its environment should manifest moral principles in every possible fashion.[11] It is during this imitative phase, when its mental processes are untrained and its awareness diminished, that the infant's consciousness is not centred in the head with its intellectual powers but rather extended into its surroundings.[12]

During the next evolutionary stage, that of Old Sun, we acquired an etheric organization in addition to that which corresponds to what is now our mineral world—although of course no such solid substance existed at that time. We not only owe our ability to grow and reproduce our species to our etheric body now in the Earth evolution, but also our faculty of ideation and memory. A proportion of the formative forces previously engaged in shaping and fashioning the physical vehicle are then made available for the forming of thoughts and other mental processes. It is easy to relate these events in a recapitulatory fashion to the stages of human development, for it is when a child's etheric body is 'born' at the time the deciduous teeth are shed that these faculties are properly made available. This marks the phase when children are ready to begin exercising their cognitive skills, their rudimentary thinking abilities. This stage corresponds to that of the Old Sun, which was marked by the introduction of the first phase of Truth, and this Verity was incorporated into us without our being in the least aware of it—'programmed' as we might say nowadays.

The shedding of the deciduous teeth marks the beginning of the second stage, when the etheric body becomes free on all sides, and is able to deploy its formative forces in developing the child's newly acquired powers of ideation and thinking, as well as that of true memory. This period of childhood is concerned with the development of the soul and therefore, as an aesthete, the child is especially open to all that is related to Beauty in all its manifestations. Significantly, pupils now become open to reason, and they should be led through feeling to appreciate its value, and this by the employment of teaching that is thoroughly imbued with an abundance of creative artistry.

The third stage of evolution was that of Old Moon, during which our astral body was added to our already existing physical and etheric organization. This Old Moon stage was not only marked by an enhancement of consciousness to that of a dreamlike nature, but also by the manifestation of the first stage of Beauty. It is then appropriate for teaching strategies to be thoroughly pervaded and infused with artistically creative methods and techniques. The period of 'gestation' of the astral body is that of childhood proper, namely, during the seven years or so between the shedding of the milk teeth and puberty. Our astral nature, which asserts itself powerfully with the onset of adolescence, is the vehicle for our life of feeling, and our aesthetic experiences are inevitably implicated in all that we recognize as art in all its forms. Our soul and our astral body are virtually identical in nature and function, and our feelings are necessarily heavily engaged in the expression of our sympathies and antipathies.

During the period of adolescence it is Truth that should actively be sought, and this by thinking, which is a spiritual activity. The more effective in a desirable sense the young person's infancy and childhood has been—in that they have been reared in a wholesome environment and brought up in a regime of kindly authority both at home and at school—the more readily amenable to the spirit of truth they are likely to be. They will probably have the advantage of being 'emotionally literate' and less prone to deviant attitudes and practices, and should therefore make better citizens, mature in their social perspectives and views concerning public welfare.

Adolescence is the time of social 'initiation' and integration, when the astral forces are at their most raw and vigorous, when human relationships with either sex are eagerly, even earnestly sought and explored. It is a critical stage in more ways than one, when parents and teachers, traditions and customs, existing social and behavioural standards—indeed 'the establishment' in all its forms—are challenged and scorned, and new ideas and response activities tested out. Yet out of this very phase of non-conformity inevitably develops a new conformity, which will of course be challenged in turn by the succeeding generation of adolescents.

Archetypal influences versus human frailty

In all this we are able to discern powerful archetypal forces at work. We come fully to appreciate that wholesome imitation in a morally rich milieu, during the stage of infancy in which the child's will-forces with their strong identification with the physical body are engaged, is entirely proper and absolutely appropriate. The stage of infancy is when the primal power of love is at its purest and most spiritual, for the new-born child will love its surroundings, and those who inhabit it, with utter devotion. During these highly formative and vulnerable years all trust, responsibility and accountability lies with the parents and significant others, and their influence is absolute. What the child experiences it in every sense *becomes*. The responsibilities of parents and teachers are of the highest possible import, for they are being inescapably obliged to 'consciously continue along the path of the gods; we take over their work of *imprinting* thought upon the brain...'[13]

The second stage of development, that of childhood proper, is when authority as such is in certain ways extended, and in others constrained. During infancy the supporting influences of the hierarchical beings are gradually withdrawn, and this in direct proportion to the rate at which the child becomes consciously aware of its environment and carers rather than unconsciously aware. Whereas previously the child absorbed its surroundings with an absolute lack of discrimination during the first seven years of development, during the second stage it is the awesome degree of responsibility of the child's significant others to *interpret* what it experiences generally. It is imperative that children grow into the world slowly, and be protected, guided and instructed in its as yet immature ways of willing, feeling and thinking. In Rudolf Steiner's own words:

> Everything is doomed to failure in education which disregards this relationship of the child to the unquestioned authority of the personality of the teacher or educator. The child must be guided in everything which he *should or should not do, think or not think, feel or not feel,* by what flows to him, by way of speech, from his teacher and educator.[14]

To many educationists and teachers, including some Waldorf teachers, this kind of 'imposition' of parent or teacher on children amounts to unforgivable 'interference' with the child's freedom, and smacks too much of indoctrination for comfort. Nevertheless, it is endorsed in archetypal terms in that the whole of humankind was so treated during the time of acquisition of our corresponding faculties during the Old Saturn, Old Sun and Old Moon evolutionary periods, when we were under the tutelage and *authority* of the spiritual powers; the precedent is undeniably there. This process is in total accord with the principle of recapitulation, and this precedent is bypassed only at considerable peril to the pupils, totally dependent as they are on their carers and significant others. Steiner was insistent that 'from the seventh year to puberty we have to do with a *child who wants to take on authority what he has to know, to feel and will'*.[15]

Nowadays, the natural kindly but firm authority which should be exercised by parents and teachers alike is not as often met with in home and school as it used to be, and excuses for this lack are abundant. However, this is to everyone's detriment for society generally, especially where human rights are involved. Rudolf Steiner, in the first lecture of *Education as a Social Problem*, makes it clear that 'people will never become ripe for these equal rights if in childhood regard for authority has not been strongly implanted ... in order to let them (children) mature for *that which is not open to argument but arises out of historical demand*'.

The emergence of the growing child into adolescence during the third seven-year period of maturation coincides with the time when freedom is warranted, namely, after puberty, when the full powers of the intellect are available for purposeful thinking, which is also extended to feeling and willing. This stage corresponds neatly with the archetypal patterns involved in the 'education' of the whole human race, for the birth of the ego in the human being at 20 or so years of age is nicely paralleled by humanity's acquisition of true freedom during the present Earth evolution of our fully developing sense of self, of egohood proper.

All change!

It is axiomatic that everything is subject to change except change itself. It is easy to overlook the fact that the members of the hierarchies above as well as below us are themselves also subject to evolutionary changes. The notion of change is of course implicit in all such words as evolution, metamorphosis, development and maturation, and these in turn imply activity of some kind, and hence the *will* of some kind of agent, whatever that agent may be. The Spirits of Will fulfilled this function at the very outset of the Old Saturn evolution, and as any agent is by definition responsible for any deeds or activities carried out, there can be no doubt as to where the factor of accountability lies. The fact remains that a doer of any deed 'flows over' in sympathetic fashion into that deed, and the changes necessarily brought about remain as it were attached to this doer, this agent, and this is how karma operates.[16] Throughout the Old Saturn, Old Sun and

Old Moon evolutions human beings were necessarily patient to the powerful spiritual agents who guided us through these stages, and so no true karma was generated.

There is a parallel to this in that just as the hierarchies made themselves responsible for our welfare and development during the Old Saturn, Old Sun and Old Moon developmental stages, a similar kind of accountability is required of all carers and teachers towards their pupils during their corresponding stages of development through infancy, childhood and adolescence. These amount to nothing else but *obligations* on their part which are awesome in their proportions, and a burden on the souls of teachers which is as daunting as it is onerous. We know that all parents, carers, teachers and significant others involved in the socialization and education of children carry on the work of the gods, and the responsibilities laid upon all individuals who become so engaged cannot in any circumstances be avoided. The implications of these responsibilities were returned to again and again by Rudolf Steiner, for once having taken them on, no one can escape them or any consequences that ensue from their activities.

Knowledge of such archetypal influences as described throughout this book, fully understood, is seen to underlie and underpin everything that Rudolf Steiner promulgated as an art of education which is grounded in the science of the spirit. If these principles are not acknowledged and implemented by educationists and teachers, the consequences cannot be attributed to the archetypal powers, who are responsible not for their implementation, but only for their provision. Here are some essential guiding thoughts which we would do well to ponder:

Each child in every age brings something new into the world from divine regions, and it is our task as educators to remove bodily and psychic obstacles out of the way; to remove hindrances so that its spirit may enter in full freedom into life. These, then, must be regarded as the three golden rules of the art of education, rules which must imbue the teacher's whole attitude and every impulse within his or her work. The golden rules which must be embraced by the teacher's and parent's whole being, and not held as theory, are: reverent gratitude to the world in the person of the child which we contemplate every day, for the child presents a problem set us by the divine worlds: thankfulness to the universe. Love for what we have to do with the child. Respect for the freedom of the child—a freedom we must not endanger; for it is to this freedom we educate the child, that it may stand in freedom in the world at our side.[17]

The Essential Threefolding of Society

*The task of the present epoch is to achieve Fraternity on the
physical plane, Liberty on the psychic plane, and Equality on
the spiritual plane.*[1]

An ideal not realized—yet

In the present Age of the Consciousness Soul it is in the
destiny of us all to become more *conscious* of what we are
doing. This is not a matter of being more intellectual or
clever, but of being increasingly aware of ourselves as
individuals and of our responsibilities in terms of social
welfare to ourselves and our fellows. Notwithstanding all the
difficulties and hindrances that will necessarily be incurred in
all this, Rudolf Steiner contended that a threefold ordering of
Society is not just another good idea—it is a demand of our
times. After considering as we have the complex nature of us
human beings, with its numerous threefold aspects, and the
unfolding of cosmic and human history, we may better
understand the seeming arrogance of his statement that such
demands are not open to question. The foundations are
already established for further future evolution and development of the Earth as well as ourselves, and all in orderly
and feasible patterns.

Such a demand included the requirement of adopting his
indications concerning the threefolding of society. During
the turbulent years which followed the First World War, he
worked with characteristic energy and zeal to disseminate his
ideas concerning the threefolding of society that would be
appropriate to sophisticated western-type civilizations. He
stressed that the ideas concerning such threefolding had
emerged directly from initiation science,[2] and needless to say

they are essentially non-political, non-ideological, and not representative of any party or faction.

As we human beings are threefold in so many ways, so this same threefolding must needs be evident in the life of society, and indeed it is in the spheres of economics, politics and civil rights. The State seeks to keep these three firmly under its influence and direction, and this constant disruption and interference by the State—or indeed a super-State in the shape of the so-called European Union—in the form of legislation, directives and suchlike lead only to equally constant turmoil and conflict. Steiner's solution to the problem was the establishment of three independently structured, autonomous 'states' within the State, representing the economic, political and cultural spheres.

Each 'state', he contended, should be free to negotiate in respect of its own interests with the other two, and ideally out of this freedom should grow mutual regard and common aims, thus contributing to a truly organic rather than mechanical unity. He claimed that such a threefolding of the body social, and the exercising of genuine freedom in its integrating and running procedures, lay as a kind of historical necessity, an inevitable future development. This must and will come, if not by peaceful negotiation and mediation then by social upheaval and violent change. The influences of the archetypes are always there, whether people are conscious of this or not; and at the same time the factor of freedom of choice is ever present, to serve egotistical or altruistic purposes as the case may be.

In April 1919 the book[3] in which he outlined his ideas was published, and in May the 'Union for the Threefold Social Order' was founded, but with the acceptance of the federal constitution of the Weimar Republic in July 1919 it had already become clear that further labours in this field would be fruitless. It is fair to say that Steiner saw the main historical task of anthroposophy as that of awakening people to the realization of their true worth as spiritual beings and disseminating ideas garnered from the spiritual world that would prevent societies from disintegrating and give foundations for a new social fabric appropriate to the changed conditions of the times.[4]

As a parallel to this, he saw the main historical task of Waldorf education as being that of providing the appropriate circumstances for human beings to attain to the optimal degree of genuine freedom which would enable them to fulfil themselves without interfering with the freedom of other members of society. He stressed that a purely intellectual approach to any kind of social problem, including that of education, was unrealistic, maintaining that our ordinary propensity for conceptual thinking is intrinsically anti-social.[5]

To state the very least, it was not by chance that Rudolf Steiner was invited by Emil Molt to found the first Waldorf School in Stuttgart, which opened its doors in September 1919. As early as 1909 his booklet *The Education of the Child in the Light of Anthroposophy* appeared, which was the substance of lectures he had previously given in various parts of Germany, and which he had recast in essay form. In it appears a statement which could easily be overlooked: 'Anthroposophical Science, *when called upon to build up an art of education*, will be able to indicate all these things in detail...' It was as though Rudolf Steiner knew that one day he would be invited to found a school based on the indications given in the booklet; and indeed he was, by Dr Emil Molt some ten years later, one destined to be the first of many. He contended that the greatest problem facing sophisticated western-type communities was that of education, and that the most difficult problem within education itself was the training of teachers. He contended that the World War occurred as the result of faulty education, for to him it was clear that if the intellectual—and thus by implication fundamentally anti-social—methods of teaching were carried on, the outlook was grim with more conflicts to follow. He forecast[6] that destructive forces would exert themselves in the future if the healing influences of the threefolding of society were not made manifest.

Significantly, in a course of lectures he gave which supplemented his book *Towards Social Renewal* he stated:

> At the foundation of the school I not only endeavoured to give shape to externals, corresponding to the requirements and the impulse of the threefold order, but I also strove to present pedagogy and didactics to the teaching staff of this new kind of school in such a light that the human being would be educated *to face life and be able to bring about a social future in accordance with certain unconquerable instincts in human nature.*[7] [My italics]

His hopes for the implementation of the principles he advocated in this book have never been realized, and although there have been numerous opportunities when they could well have been implemented, they have never even been considered.

Archetypal principles and social problems

There are sound archetypal reasons why such a patterning of the body social should—indeed, must—eventually come about. This is all part of the ongoing process of achieving one of the main goals of our Earthly development, namely, to render ourselves free and independent.[8] In the table below the order of bestowal of our present soul-qualities and of the Verities has been followed. However, the 'reversal factor', which has been discussed in other contexts, is also seen to be present. For instance, our constitutional vehicles (a), our states of consciousness (b), our soul faculties (c) appear in order of *descent*, from Old Saturn to Old Sun and Old Moon. However, the corresponding Verities (d) appear in reverse order of conferral, and this arrangement is entirely appropriate, as discussed in Chapter 4 and elsewhere.

Conferred principles and their features				*Their expression within society*		
(a)	(b)	(c)	(d)	(e)	(f)	(g)
Body	Sleeping	Willing	Goodness	Fraternity	Economics	Socialism
Soul	Dreaming	Feeling	Beauty	Equality	Rights	Democracy
Spirit	Waking	Thinking	Truth	Liberty	Cultural	Individualism

Enough has been said about the principles listed at (a), (b), (c) and (d)—and there could have been more[9]—but the main purpose at present is to indicate how our soul-faculties of thinking, feeling and willing find expression in the countless national and racial communities and their 'education' in terms of the advancement of world civilization in general. The nine factors listed under (e), (f) and (g) must to a considerable extent be regarded as being potential and provisional in their nature and manner of implementation, for this depends on the actions of future generations. A brief discussion of their many-faceted characteristics is nevertheless warranted.

The three great ideals of Fraternity, Equality and Liberty which were proclaimed with such violence at the time of the French Revolution are those by which western civilization has progressed, however stormily, and by which future progress will be made. Rudolf Steiner had some interesting observations to make concerning the origins of these three ideals in Freemasonry in connection with the Grail and the three 'pillars of society', namely, Wisdom, Beauty and Strength, which comprise the three principles associated with the 'Royal Art':

> ... today the first dawn is already beginning for the use of these living forces in the affairs of social life; that is the real secret surrounding the Grail. The last event brought about in the social sphere by the old Freemasonry was the French Revolution, in which the basic idea of the old Freemasonry came into the open in the social sphere with the ideas of equality, liberty and fraternity as its corollaries. Whoever knows this also knows that the ideas which emanated from the Grail were propagated through innumerable channels, and constituted the really active force in the French Revolution ... The Royal Art will in the future be a social art.[10]

In these three principles, which were of course united at that time in history, it is easy to recognize science and art, but Rudolf Steiner related Strength to the State and the powers attaching to it. However, it is easy to connect Strength with the authority of the god-kings and priest-kings of those ancient times who ideally sustained Goodness with that Strength, and 'the divine right of kings' which marked the gradual transition from their era through feudal and similar times to modern democratic procedures. However unsatisfactory these are in fulfilling the maxim *Vox populi, vox Dei*, the voice of God is seldom heard in modern parliamentary and governmental palaces today.

However, it is undeniable that as ideals they form the fabric of our culture within society, and sure enough they match and reflect the threefoldness of the human constitution in intricate detail. The concept of Liberty obviously has close relationships with our ego, for freedom of *thought* must, to be effective, be expressed as freedom of action, but this with regard for the freedom of others, which is primarily facilitated by the will. Apart from engaging our *spirit*, other relating factors are our spiritual or *cultural* life as well as that of *individualism* (and by implication freedom), and these are discernible from the foregoing table. These two are clearly related, for much in the sphere of culture is achieved by individual effort rather than by committee.

Freedom inheres in individual behaviour, and Liberty in that of society at large. Needless to say, all this implies the workings of karma and reincarnation, for freedom of action, which is implicit in all self-development, necessarily involves our spirit-filled ego, itself deathless. It is abundantly clear that this can only be achieved by progressing through a series of re-embodiments, to which birth and death merely mark the boundaries of our Earthly and Heavenly existence. It is reasonable to contend that, of the three great Ideals, it is the one of which we are most conscious, and concerning which most progress has been made within western-type civilizations.

There can be no Equality within society without its acknowledgement by us and our fellows of the *rights* of each individual member. Cynics contend that there is no such thing as true equality, and not even equality of opportunity. It is fairly easy to recognize within society the men of gold, the men of silver, the men of bronze and the men of dross, and some individuals are indeed more equal than others. Connections with the life of the soul are not difficult to discern. We share the astrality of the whole cosmos, the commonality of human emotional life, the swings of sympathy and antipathy, and every shade of *feeling* with every other person in the whole world.

It is in this realm of the *soul* that we are most truly human, and it is within this domain that negotiation concerning political issues is to a great extent carried on. This is the region of opinion rather than fact, of biased views and one-sided argument, emotive persuasion rather than reference to cold fact. This notion of harmoniousness, reasonableness, of overall balance, has been touched on elsewhere in connection with the Verity of Beauty, and it finds echoes when, in our passage through the soul world after death, we are obliged to face those imbalances we fostered during our previous Earthly life. The pluses and minuses eventually balance themselves out, thus realizing the *equals*. It can be readily acknowledged from recognition of these inter-relationships that the notions of Equality and *democracy* are also closely involved.

True to the dual orientation of the soul, expressed in our life of feeling as alternation between sympathy and antipathy, affirmation and denial, attachment and detachment and so on, its association with democracy is not to be denied. This is expressed in the process whereby individuals, in casting their vote, subordinate their will to that of the majority. The situation is as unavoidable as it is paradoxical; the expression of individualism leads to its inevitable suppression, the aim being the ensuring of the maximal good for the greatest number. So there we have a compromise between the 'reasonable compulsion' of socialism and the egotistical pitfalls inherent in individualism. The way forward is to respond to the impulse emanating from the Christ, who does not compel but rather, as a truly compassionate Big Brother, attracts us all to a *genuine* brand of socialism.

It may seem strange at first sight that it is our bodily nature that is essentially implicated with the ideal of Fraternity, the machinations of economics, and the ethos of Socialism—but this in terms of its broad application rather than those of any political party. The notion of brotherhood is of course a very old one, but in the past it has borne connotations of blood-relationship and coteries rather than those of a universalistic nature. The ideal of universal fellowship, though widely acknowledged as being supremely worthy and desirable, is nonetheless at a positively embryonic stage in terms of achievement. What really counts is its manifestation in the world as Goodness, which is the Verity most connected with altruism and fellow-feeling and the soul-faculty of *willing*. Goodness is representative of love in action, deeds performed by the agency of human limbs, hence the undoubted connections with our *bodily* vehicle.

Economics is very far from being a 'science', for in many respects it is dependent not so much on laws and principles as on the sentiments of money-grubbers and the constraints of market forces. It has seen its development almost wholly during our present Age of the Consciousness Soul in that this has taken place since the fifteenth century with the dramatic spurt since then of science and technology, world-wide trading and commerce, and so on. Arguments for and against free (market) or command national and international economies all too often exclude factors which should indeed be paramount, namely, those involving social values and the general welfare of society.

Rudolf Steiner set out this *fundamental social law*, derived directly from spiritual science, redolent of a genuine *pro bono publico* ethos:

> In a community of human beings working together, the well-being of the community will be the greater the less the individual claims for himself the proceeds of the work he himself has done;

that is to say, the more of these proceeds he makes over to his fellow-workers, and the more of his requirements are met, not out of his own work done, but out of the work done by others.[11]

In the grasping, competitive, ambitious and thoroughly materialistic climate so prevalent today, such principles seem unrealistic, to say the very least. However his social law is there, his writings and lecture courses on the Threefold Social Order are there, to be turned to in desperation some time in the future when intellectually arrived at 'solutions' arrived at in 'think tanks' are seen still to be failing, even as they are failing us now.

Problems of socialization and education

As we have seen, a thorough knowledge and appreciation of the archetypes and their manifest influences in both spiritual and natural worlds is clearly apparent in Steiner's whole philosophy and its practical application in many and diverse areas. Initiatives involving what he called the 'children of the Being Anthroposophia', namely, those of medicine, agriculture, education, architecture and the arts generally, have been particularly successful. But his attempts immediately after the First World War at interesting the general public in Germany as well as leading political figures of the time in his ideas concerning the Threefold Social Order failed. These took full account of the relevant archetypal principles, but sound as they were from every point of view, and acknowledged as such by various individuals in positions of power and authority in Germany, they were not implemented. Doing so would have required considerable courage and tenacity of purpose on the part of governments and administrators, and these qualities were clearly lacking then, and they are now.

As mentioned elsewhere, our soul-forces of thinking, feeling and willing are becoming more and more independent of one another, in parallel with the process of the splitting up of the three corresponding Verities and the three main areas of activity embracing science, art and religion. The three main spheres in which the ideals underlying the concept of threefolding in society operate are Fraternity, Equality and Liberty. Economic, political and the cultural activities run parallel to these, as do their corresponding ideologies, which are represented in socialism, democracy and individualism, all respectively, as follows:

(Imitation)	Fraternity	Economic	Socialism
(Authority)	Equality	Political	Democracy
(Freedom)	Liberty	Cultural	Individualism

The pedagogical modes associated with these main areas can be seen to correspond to the three stages of infancy, childhood, and adolescence. These in turn are, as we have seen, related to the development of willing, feeling and thinking, based on the archetypal agencies of Goodness, Beauty and Truth, and body, soul and spirit, all respectively. All these factors are thus interconnected in various ways, the whole forming a convincing model of the human being as an individual and of the basic structure of society. In these connections Rudolf Steiner had this to say:

> Upon this threefold educational basis must be erected what is to flourish for man's future. If we do not know that the physical body must become an imitator in the right way we shall merely implant animal instincts in this body. If we are now aware that between the seventh and the fourteenth years the etheric body passes through a special development that must be based on authority, there will develop in man merely a cultural drowsiness, and the force needed for the rights organism will not be present. If from the fifteenth year onward we do not infuse all education with the power of love that is bound up with the astral body, men will never be able to develop their astral bodies into independent beings. These things intertwine. Therefore I must say:
>
> > Proper imitation develops freedom;
> > Authority develops the rights life;
> > Brotherliness, love, develops the economic life.

But turned about it is also true. When love is not developed in the right way freedom is lacking; and when imitation is not developed in the right way, animal instincts grow rampant.[12]

In this passage and with reference to the Table set out above he appears to contradict himself, for earlier in the same lecture he said:

Adults will have to live in a social organism which, in regard to the economic aspect, will be social; in regard to government, democratic, and from the spiritual aspect, liberal, free. The great problem of the future will be that of education.[13]

Here we have an apparent contradiction, for earlier in the lecture Rudolf Steiner explained why it is that an infant is an imitator; that while in the spiritual worlds before conception, the unborn child imitates beings of the higher hierarchies among whom it is living, and with whom, in a certain sense, it is united, and that after it is born it continues to imitate in its Earthly environment. He went on:

For men will have to make clear to themselves that when the children are grown to adulthood in the social organism they will have to be free beings, and one can become free only if as a child one has been a most intensive imitator. This natural power of a child must be strongly developed precisely for the time when socialism will break in upon us.[14]

Steiner was careful to point out that what he meant by 'socialism' has strictly to do with the Economic State in the sense of the Threefold Social Order, and not in any sense of party-political socialism. It may well be that here, however, he had in mind political connotations, for in the same lecture he stated clearly that 'socialism can only refer to the economic life, democracy only to the sphere of civil rights, and individualism would refer to the spiritual life'.[15]

Waldorf principles and their social implications

The supporting structure of Steiner pedagogy in all its ramifications is in many respects complex and intricate, but its three main pillars are undoubtedly those of Imitation, Authority and Freedom. These represent the three pedagogical modes for the three seven-year human developmental stages of infancy, childhood and adolescence, all of which have been vindicated by illustration, characterization and argument in earlier chapters. The table on p. 130 asserts that Goodness is associated with our infant stage, and also with Fraternity; and correspondingly, childhood with Beauty and Equality, and Truth with Freedom and Liberty after adolescence. Goodness and Truth have long been incorporated into the life of human communities and society in general. These for the most part have their basis in religion, and certainly in Christianity, as reflection will confirm. Deviations or aberrations which were formerly considered as departing from these conventional values have nevertheless become established as behavioural norms, whether or not regarded as anti-social in essence, and these include climbing crime rates, drug abuse, promiscuity and falling moral standards generally.

A very serious problem in western countries arises from the fact that the results of imitation in infancy can be seen to be, in many respects, the polar opposite of the practice of freedom, which is the societal attribute associated with adolescence. Whatever is imprinted upon the children of today by reason of the conditioning effects of socialization and education—in short, all that comes under the heading of imitation—is brought into opposition to what emerges during the usual maturational processes of adolescence, when the right to freedom is the accepted norm in terms of mores, and hence as norm-al. Thus adolescents are necessarily faced with the tremendous conflicts and tensions involved in the struggle to reconcile all that has been imprinted on them during infancy and childhood, which manifests as compulsive attitudes and behaviour, with the overwhelming urge towards freedom of action in adolescence and adulthood.

We have seen how it comes about that unless the requisite degree of discipline is exercised, attainment to the Verity of Truth cannot be accomplished; and so it is with the achievement of Freedom. It is a truism that genuine freedom is the luxury of self-discipline, but the kind of freedom experienced after release from a regime of kindly authority, represented by our being subjected to the tutelage of the Hierarchies in terms of human evolution when we had no choice, corresponds to the release of pupils after puberty after seven years of being subject to the kindly authority of their class teachers. The kind of spurious freedom associated with *laissez-faire* attitudes is clearly discernible in much of mainstream education with its accent on 'free expression', self-chosen programmes of learning, 'research projects' and other so-called pupil-centred methodologies.

By the time of the founding of the first Waldorf school in 1919 it was clear to Rudolf Steiner that his ideas regarding a Threefold Social Order had not met with the response he had hoped for. Needless to say, the links between these ideas and those on education are very strong, and plenty of evidence of this has been given elsewhere. The following educational principles suggest that he wished for Waldorf school leavers to be creators of a humane and caring society:

> Today children are educated [in orthodox intellectual fashion] in a way that does not awaken in them the forces that make individuals strong for life. People become strong through being an imitator up to their seventh year; through following a worthy authority up to their fourteenth year; and through the fact that their capacity for love is developed in the right way up to their twenty-first year. Later on this strength cannot be developed. What a person lacks because the forces were not awakened which should have been awakened in definite periods of childhood—this is what makes him or her a problem-filled nature. *This fact must be made known!*[16]

Apparent contradictions such as those indicated provide

yet another example of the dangers involved in applying our ordinary intellectual powers of analysis, logical sequences of thought, deduction and suchlike to principles obtaining in the supersensory realms. It is always necessary to bear in mind the dynamic character of spiritual processes, which do not always correspond with or respond to our ways of thinking normally associated with the laws and workings which characterize those of the external, material world, and a kind of vigilant sensitivity needs to be fostered at all times. As ever, people must make up their own minds in face of seeming contradiction, but reconciliation is invariably possible. It is essential that we maintain mobility of thinking, at the same time searching diligently for solutions to our difficulties.

For example, on 19 October 1918, Rudolf Steiner declared that the task of the present Age of the Consciousness Soul 'is to achieve Fraternity on the physical plane, Liberty on the psychic plane, and Equality on the spiritual plane', and this statement, culled from his lecture cycle *From Symptom to Reality in Modern History,* was adopted as the thematic quotation for this chapter. During his second lecture of this course he pointed out briefly that, whereas it is perfectly possible to achieve Fraternity on the physical level, namely, in connection with community and social life, it would be a mistake to imagine that Liberty may be achieved by the individual at this level; rather must it be at the soul level.

However, on 9 August 1919, in the first lecture of *Education as a Social Problem*, he set out in detail arguments to the effect that although Fraternity can be achieved on the physical plane, Equality can be achieved *only* on the soul or psychic plane, and Liberty on the spiritual plane, and not vice versa, as he had stated in the previous assertion. Steiner's inconsistency in these two contentions are nonetheless more apparent than real; for in practical life freedom and equality are virtually reciprocal and complementary, as are the functions of our soul and spirit. His great concern was that the great ideals of Fraternity, Equality and Liberty should not be seized and applied indiscriminately to human affairs, but be properly applied both to Threefold Man and to Threefold Society: Fraternity to the physical plane and Equality and Liberty to the soul-spiritual planes.[17]

Steiner insisted that socialism for the economic life, democracy for the life of rights, and individualism for life of the spirit are historical demands. Hence his pedagogical principles which aim at fostering these forces and qualities also 'are not open to argument, but arise as historical demand'. These apparently brash, presumptuous and uncompromising statements were not substantiated at the time, but it is always helpful to treat spiritual-scientific truths and principles as concrete realities, never as abstract notions, and much less as mere opinion. Evidence that certain social demands are valid can be gathered from the various evolutionary and historical events and concerns discussed in previous chapters. The rationales for his emphasis on the crucial importance for infants to be brought up by kindly, loving and caring parents and significant others who are able to provide a wholesome environment that is worthy of strong and consistent imitation are clearly discernible. Likewise, the need for kindly and dependable authority figures during their childhood years can clearly be seen to be essential for individual and social health and welfare, and really do represent genuine and valid *demands* which are indeed not 'open to argument'.

Future prospects

Looking forward to the Sixth Epoch,[18] Rudolf Steiner asserted that the threefolding principle so characteristic of not only ourselves in our very constitution, but also in the manifestation of our behaviour in societal terms, would continue to hold. With regard to our fraternal propensities which, in terms of the Threefold Social Order, would have ties with genuine socialism coming about with special reference to economic affairs, he could foresee a further development of these factors within society. He contended that brotherliness among peoples would develop into recognition of the innate character of all individuals for what they are, namely, as beings of spiritual origin and nature rather than creatures who had evolved from primitive organisms which— inexplicably—emerged from the primeval ooze.

He also contended that through a process of metamorphosis and further advancement in terms of equal democratic rights, with the concomitant attributes of these extending to equality of opportunity, there would develop a widespread tolerance of all religions of whatever origins and character, so that complete freedom in all matters involving people's religious lives would come about. Moreover, he envisaged a deepening of the understanding and purposes of Christianity into a worldwide appreciation of complete freedom in the whole area of religious beliefs and convictions.

All this is of course according to the Grand Plan, and there is little point in going into the details of what might be. The potentialities have already been outlined, and these will come about only if humanity has the will to realize them. We may well benefit from pondering the message given by Rudolf Steiner in these lines:

In the boundless Without
Find thyself, O Man!

In the innermost Within
Feel the boundless Worlds!

So will it be revealed:
Nowhere the Riddle of Worlds is solved,
Save in the being of Man.[19]

Appendix

Causality and the Factor of Change

As sentient and rational beings we acknowledge that we are part of the Universal Whole, and are subject to its laws, whether we regard ourselves either as seeking to read the thoughts of the Creator or investigating the complexities of nature and its mechanisms. We all possess the innate urge to understand Nature and make sense of what goes on in and around us as well as the desire to change things to suit our wishes and needs, and in this sense we too are creative.

Moreover, with every law and principle we have been able to discover and verify, it becomes ever clearer that order and regularity rule, and this gives us confidence in nature and its manifold purposes. By application of the basic principles of scientific investigation—observation and experiment—we have been increasingly capable of bringing about changes in ourselves and our environment. Thus we fulfil the role of agents (as active causes) and discharge our responsibilities for activating the appropriate agencies (as instrumental forces responsible for effecting the appropriate results).

Such consequences are a necessary product of this process of *change* which is evidenced by reason of an 'event' or occurrence. In this respect everyday language usage is loose enough—inaccurate enough—to be misleading as to the truth of the matter. People often say 'Times change', thus employing the active voice in terms of grammar, whereas employment of the passive voice is more proper, and certainly more legitimate. 'Times' never 'change' of themselves; *times are changed*—by reason of actions by the relevant 'change agents'.

In present circumstances, which represent the current stage of evolution, human beings are well placed to bring about certain changes in the natural world, adapting its resources to suit real or supposed needs as far as its laws will allow. In the final analysis, it is our will-driven ego, in response to the urge to satisfy some real or imagined need, which represents the *cause* of every deed effected by every human being. We are well motivated to change things to suit ourselves in the short term, whether or not we are aware of the consequences in the longer term.

The performance of every act, function or operation necessarily alters existing conditions, and change is thereby brought about. As every deed requires an agent to effect it, a pattern of threefolding emerges; for there must be involved: (a) that which is subject to change, as patient; (b) that which brings about the change, as agent, and (c) the result. An agent cannot qualify as such until the deed has been done, a change of some kind has taken place, and what is in technical or philosophical terms an 'event' has occurred. The bringing about of this event, which comprises the involvement of the three factors already described, thus establishes threefolding as a principle.

Of necessity, therefore, a field of operation exists between the agent and the patient, as between two poles: the agent is active, the patient passive, and the effect is the product or yield. This process is entirely logical and consistent. Thus we have life, death and what occurs between; giver, gift and recipient; speaker, what is uttered and hearer, and so on. An obvious paradigm of this principle of threefolding is apparent in language usage in the proper arrangement of subject, object and verb (the 'doing word'), as predicating the inter-action or relationship between the two. In grammar, a subject must be predicated in order to make sense, and a predicate cannot stand alone and be completely meaningful. Hence it is clear that the basic structure of language itself rests on the model of threefolding.

We are therefore able to confirm the rule of threefolding as standard in respect of every action. On these grounds, we may justifiably regard Nature in all its manifold functions thus: the unmanifest as archetype, the manner in which it operates, and the manifest product. Where matters of cause and effect are concerned, it is imperative to bear in mind that the processes involving the 'laws of nature' are entirely mechanical; the principle of morality, and hence that of Justice as an archetype, is not involved in these. As discussed in Chapter 4, the universal law of self-correction applies to human beings only, and not to inanimate objects, or even animals.

However, as hinted earlier, there may well be latent as well as manifest functions attaching to the deeds of human beings—an intriguing notion indeed where karma or self-created destiny is involved—and these are by definition bound to effect some kind of *change*. It is beyond argument that the primal Verity of Justice is inextricably involved in all human actions in which issues of moral consequence are implicated, and of necessity these entail spiritual rather than mechanical laws. In the following statement by Rudolf Steiner this notion as well as the functions of agent, patient and operational field linking the two are clearly discernible:

> Unless a result is produced which reacts upon the being or thing producing it; unless there is this peculiar reacting effect upon the being which caused it, the idea of karma is not to be thought of.[1]

Notes

Thematic quote on title page: Rudolf Steiner, *Verses and Meditations*, p. 110.

Chapter 1   Agents, Agencies and Archetypes **(pages 3–12)**

1 Steiner, R., *Riddle of Humanity*, lecture 12.
2 Steiner, R., *Theosophy*, Chapter 3, p. 145f.
3 Steiner, R., *Lucifer and Ahriman, passim. Man as a Picture of the Living Spirit*, lecture of 2 September 1923. See also Childs, G., *An Imp on Either Shoulder*, Fire Tree Press, *passim*.
4 Steiner, R., *A Theory of Knowledge Implicit in Goethe's World-Conception, passim*.
5 Steiner, R., 'Measure, Number and Weight—Weightless Colour', lecture 11 (29 July 1923), in *Colour*.

Chapter 2   Driving Forces in World Evolution **(pages 13–28)**

1 Steiner, R., *Verses and Meditations*, p. 97.
2 Steiner, R., *Spiritual Hierarchies and the Physical World*, lecture 10.
3 Steiner, R., ibid., lecture 3.
4 Steiner, R., *The Influence of Spiritual Beings upon Man*, lecture 10.
5 Steiner, R., *The Kingdom of Childhood*, lecture 2.
6 O'Connor, D.J., *Free Will*, Macmillan, 1972, *passim*.
7 Steiner, R., *Cosmic Memory*, Chapter 11.

Chapter 3   The Course of Western Civilization **(pages 29–42)**

1 Steiner, R., *The Shaping of Our Destiny*, lecture of 6 April 1923.
2 Steiner, R., *Anthroposophical Leading Thoughts*, p. 142.
3 Steiner, R., ibid., p. 145.
4 Wachsmuth, G., *The Evolution of Mankind*, Philosophical-Anthroposophical Press, 1961.
5 Cloos, W., *The Living Earth*, Lanthorn Press, 1977. Note: For comprehensive discussion, see Childs, G., *5 + 7 = 12 Senses*, Fire Tree Press.

6 Steiner, R., *The Mission of Anger*, lecture of 21 October 1909.
7 Steiner, R., *The Threefold Social Order, The Threefold Order of the Body Social*, Study Series I, II, III. See also Gulbekian, S., *At the Grave of Civilization?* Temple Lodge Publishing.
8 Steiner, R., *Education as a Social Problem*. See also Childs, G., *Education and Beyond*, Floris Books.
9 Steiner, R., *The Course of My Life*, passim.
10 Steiner, R., Address to the General Anthroposophical Society, 25 December 1923. See also Grosse, R., *The Living Being Anthroposophia*. Note: The 'Being Anthroposophia' referred to in these contexts should not be confused with the entity of the same name which is under discussion in Sergei O. Prokofieff's book *The Heavenly Sophia and the Being Anthroposophia*, Temple Lodge, 1996.
11 Steiner, R., *Three Phases in the Work of Anthroposophy*.
12 Steiner, R., *Occult Movements in the Nineteenth Century*.
13 Steiner, R., *A Modern Art of Education*, lecture 2.

Chapter 4   Truth, Beauty and Goodness as Archetypal Principles **(pages 43–62)**

1 Steiner, R., *The Riddle of Humanity*, lecture 5.
2 Steiner, R., *Theosophy*, Chapter 3.
3 Steiner, R., *Truth, Beauty and Goodness*, lecture of 19 January 1923.
4 Steiner, R., *The Mission of Art*, lecture of 12 May 1910.
5 Read, H., *The Meaning of Art*, p. 20.
6 Read, H., ibid, p. 196.
7 Note: But see also Chapter 7 for further discussion.
8 Steiner, R., *The Inner Nature of Man and Life after Death*, lecture 5.
9 Steiner, R., *The Riddle of Humanity*, lecture 5.
10 Steiner, R., *The Inner Nature of Man and Life after Death*, lecture 4.
11 Steiner, R., *The Riddle of Humanity*, lecture 12.
12 Steiner, R., *Guidance in Esoteric Training*, p. 38.
13 Steiner, R., 'The Nature of Egotism', lecture in *Metamorphoses of the Soul*.

14 Steiner, R., *Man as Picture of the Living Spirit*, lecture of 2 September 1923.
15 Steiner, R., ibid.
16 Note: For fuller discussion, see Childs, G., *From Birthlessness to Deathlessness*, Fire Tree Press.
17 Steiner, R., *Truth, Beauty and Goodness*.
18 Steiner, R., 'Measure, Number and Weight—Weightless Colour', lecture 11 (29 July 1923), in *Colour*.
19 Steiner, R., *The Christ Impulse and the Development of Ego-Consciousness*, lectures of 2 and 8 May 1910. See also the *Orestian Trilogy* of Aeschylus.
20 Steiner, R., *The Philosophy of Freedom*.

Chapter 5 The Eternal Verities and Society **(pages 63–84)**

1 Steiner, R., *Man and the World of the Stars*, lecture 5.
2 Steiner, R., *Education for Adolescence*, lecture 12.
3 Steiner, R., *The Mission of Art*, lecture of 12 May 1910.
4 Steiner, R., 'Measure, Number and Weight—Weightless Colour', lecture 11 (29 July 1923), in *Colour*.
5 Steiner, R., *The Spiritual Hierarchies and the Physical World*, lecture 4.
6 Steiner, R., *The Riddle of Humanity*, lecture 4.
7 Steiner, R., ibid.
8 Steiner, R., *The Closing of the Spiritual Worlds to Humanity during the Post-Atlantean Development*, lecture of 25 December 1916.
9 Steiner, R., 'The Mission of Truth', lecture of 22 October 1909 in *Metamorphoses of the Soul*.
10 Steiner, R., *Guidance in Esoteric Training*.
11 Steiner, R., 'The Mission of Truth', in *Metamorphoses of the Soul*.
12 Steiner, R., 'Measure, Number and Weight—Weightless Colour', lecture 11 (29 July 1923), in *Colour*.
13 Steiner, R., *The Spiritual Guidance of Mankind*, lecture 1.
14 Steiner, R., *The Roots of Education*, lecture 5.
15 Steiner, R., *Truth, Beauty and Goodness*.
16 Steiner, R., 'Measure, Number and Weight—Weightless Colour', lecture 11 (29 July, 1923), in *Colour*.
17 Steiner, R., ibid.

Chapter 6   Foundations of Thinking, Feeling and Willing
(pages 85–104)

1 Steiner, R., *Verses and Meditations*, p. 111.
2 Steiner, R., 'The Hierarchies and the Nature of the Rainbow', lecture 12 (4 January 1924), in *Colour*.
3 Steiner, R., *Spiritual Hierarchies and the Physical World*, lecture 5.
4 Steiner, R., ibid, lecture 10.
5 Steiner, R., ibid, lecture 3.
6 Steiner, R., *Verses and Meditations*, p. 59.
7 Steiner, R., *Anthroposophical Leading Thoughts*, Nos 59, 60, 61.
8 Note: The term 'monad', commonly attributed to Leibniz, and referring to a 'permanent atom' in rather a material sense, was employed by Rudolf Steiner during the early years of the twentieth century. The concept is difficult to define, but presumably what he meant to convey was the idea of *an elementary indivisible spiritual substance* that functions as a 'spiritual seed', which is the expression he tended to employ later.
9 Steiner, R., See *Life Beyond Death; The Forming of Destiny and the Life after Death; Life between Death and Rebirth*.
10 Steiner, R., *The Wisdom of Man, of the Soul, and of the Spirit*, lecture of 1 November 1910, Berlin.
11 Steiner, R., *Study of Man*, lecture 5.
12 Steiner, R., ibid.
13 Steiner, R., ibid, lecture 6.
14 Steiner, R., *Riddle of Humanity*, lecture 12.
15 Steiner, R., *Earthly and Cosmic Man*, lecture 6.
16 Steiner, R., ibid.
17 Steiner, R., *Social and Antisocial Impulses in Humanity*, Berne, lecture of 12 December 1918.
18 Steiner, R., *The Influence of Spiritual Beings upon Man*, lecture 7.
19 Steiner, R., *Earthly and Cosmic Man*, lecture 6.
20 Steiner, R., *Verses and Meditations*, p. 190.
21 Steiner, R., ibid.
22 Steiner, R., *The Temple Legend*, lecture 20 (2 January 1906).

Chapter 7   Steiner Education as a Demand of the Age
(pages 105–120)

1 Steiner, R., *Truth Wrought Words*, p. 13.
2 Steiner, R., *The Roots of Education*, lecture 1.
3 Steiner, R., *Study of Man*, lecture 1.
4 Steiner, R., *Theosophy*, Chapter 3.
5 Steiner, R., *Study of Man*, lecture 3.
6 Steiner, R., *Education for Adolescence*, lecture 7.
7 Steiner, R., *Education as a Social Problem*, lecture 5.
8 Steiner, R., *The Riddle of Humanity*, lecture 6.
9 Steiner, R., *Study of Man*, lecture 1.
10 Steiner, R., *Occult Science—an Outline*.
11 Steiner, R., *The Kingdom of Childhood*, lecture 2.
12 Steiner, R., *The Roots of Education*, lecture 2; *Education for Adolescence*, lecture 8.
13 Steiner, R., *Supersensible Physiology*, lecture of 21 September 20.
14 Steiner, R., *Human Values in Education*, lecture 3. See also Childs, G., *Education and Beyond*, Chapter 11.
15 Steiner, R., *Study of Man*, lecture 9.
16 Steiner, R., *Theosophy*, Chapter 2.
17 Steiner, R., *The Spiritual Ground of Education*, lecture 4.

Chapter 8   The Essential Threefolding of Society **(pages 121–136)**

1 Steiner, R., *From Symptom to Reality in Modern History*, lecture 2.
2 Steiner, R., *The Meaning of the Concept of Threefolding for Our Time*, lecture of 11 April 1919.
3 Steiner, R., *The Threefold Commonwealth*, available now as *Towards Social Renewal*.
4 Steiner, R., *Spiritual-scientific Treatment of Social and Pedagogical Problems*, lecture of 22 June 1919.
5 Hahn, H., 'The Birth of the Waldorf School from the Threefold Social Movement', in von Poturzyn, M., *Rudolf Steiner: Recollections by Some of His Pupils*, 1958.
6 Steiner, R., *The Cosmic New Year*, lecture 4.
7 Steiner, R., *The Social Future*, Anthroposophic Press, 1972, lecture 4.
8 Steiner, R., *The Shaping of our Destiny*, lecture of 16 April 1923.

9 Childs, G., *Education and Beyond*, Floris Books, Chapters 10 and 11.
10 Steiner, R., 'The Royal Art in a New Form', lecture 20 (2 January 1906), in *The Temple Legend*.
11 Steiner, R., *Anthroposophy and the Social Question*.
12 Steiner, R., *Education as a Social Problem*, lecture 1.
13 Steiner, R., ibid.
14 Steiner, R., ibid.
15 Steiner, R., ibid.
16 Steiner, R., ibid, lecture 2.
17 Steiner, R., ibid, lecture 1.
18 Steiner, R., *Preparing for the Sixth Epoch*.
19 Steiner, R., *Verses and Meditations*, p. 49.

Appendix: Causality and the Factor of Change **(pages 137–139)**

1 Steiner, R., *Manifestations of Karma*, lecture 1. See also Chapter 2 of *Theosophy* for further discussion.

Select Bibliography

Books by Rudolf Steiner

Address to the General Anthroposophical Society, 25 December 1923, now *The Christmas Conference*, Anthroposophic Press, 1990

Anthroposophy and the Social Question, Mercury Press, 1982

Anthroposophical Leading Thoughts, Rudolf Steiner Press, 1998, as *Letters to the Members*, Rudolf Steiner Publishing Co, n.d.

Christ Impulse and the Development of Ego-Consciousness, Anthroposophical Publishing Co, 1926

Cosmic Memory, Rudolf Steiner Publications, 1959

Cosmic New Year, Percy Lund, Humphries, 1932

Course of My Life, Anthroposophic Press, 1951

Earthly and Cosmic Man, Rudolf Steiner Publishing Co, 1948

Education as a Social Problem, Anthroposophic Press, 1969

Forming of Destiny and the Life after Death, Anthroposophical Publishing Co, 1927

From Symptom to Reality in Modern History, Rudolf Steiner Press, 1976

Guidance in Esoteric Training, Rudolf Steiner Press, 1994

'Hierarchies and the Nature of the Rainbow', in *Colour*, Rudolf Steiner Press, 1992

Human Values in Education, Rudolf Steiner Press, 1971

Influence of Spiritual Beings upon Man, Anthroposophic Press, 1961

Inner Nature of Man and Life after Death, Anthroposophical Publishing Co, 1928

Kingdom of Childhood, Rudolf Steiner Press, 1964

Life Between Death and Rebirth, Anthroposophic Press, 1968

Life Beyond Death, Rudolf Steiner Press, 1995

Lucifer and Ahriman, Rudolf Steiner Publishing Co, 1947

Man and the World of the Stars, Anthroposophic Press, 1963

Man as a Picture of the Living Spirit, Rudolf Steiner Press, 1972

Manifestations of Karma, Rudolf Steiner Publishing Co, 1947

'Measure, Number and Weight—Weightless Colour', in *Colour*, Rudolf Steiner Press, 1992

'Mission of Anger' in *Metamorphoses of the Soul*, Rudolf Steiner Publishing Co, n.d.

'Mission of Art' in *Metamorphoses of the Soul*

'Mission of Truth' in *Metamorphoses of the Soul*

A Modern Art of Education (*Education and Modern Spiritual Life*, Rudolf Steiner Press, 1954)

'Nature of Egotism' in *Metamorphoses of the Soul*

Occult Movements in the Nineteenth Century, Rudolf Steiner Press, 1973

Occult Science—an Outline, Anthroposophic Press, 1939

Philosophy of Freedom, Rudolf Steiner Press, 1970

Preparing for the Sixth Epoch, Anthroposophic Press, 1957

Riddle of Humanity, Rudolf Steiner Press, 1990

Roots of Education, Rudolf Steiner Press, 1968

'Royal Art in a New Form', in *The Temple Legend*, Rudolf Steiner Press, 1985

'Shaping of Our Destiny', in *Angels*, Rudolf Steiner Press, 1996

Social Future, Anthroposophic Press, 1972

Spiritual Ground of Education, Anthroposophic Publishing Co, 1947

Spiritual Guidance of Mankind, Rudolf Steiner Publishing Co, n.d.

Spiritual Hierarchies and the Physical World, Anthroposophic Press, 1996

Study of Man, Rudolf Steiner Publishing Co, 1947

Supersensible Physiology, Anthroposophic Press, 1945

Temple Legend, Rudolf Steiner Press, 1985

Theory of Knowledge Implicit in Goethe's World-Conception, Anthroposophic Press, 1940

Theosophy, Anthroposophic Press, 1946

Threefold Order of the Body Social, Study Series I, II, III. Cyclostyled, n.d.

Threefold Social Order, now *Towards Social Renewal*, Rudolf Steiner Press, 1977

Truth, Beauty and Goodness, Rudolf Steiner Publishing Co, 1927

Truth-Wrought Words, Anthroposophic Press, 1979

Verses and Meditations, Rudolf Steiner Press, 1979

Waldorf Education for Adolescence, Kolisko Archives Publications, 1980

Wisdom of Man, of the Soul, and of the Spirit, Anthroposophic Press, 1971

References in the text are to the above editions. For current books by Rudolf Steiner contact Rudolf Steiner Press, London or Anthroposophic Press, New York

Books by other authors

Childs G., *An Imp on Either Shoulder*, Fire Tree Press, 1995

Childs G., *5 + 7 = 12 Senses*, Fire Tree Press, 1996

Childs G., *From Birthlessness to Deathlessness*, Fire Tree Press, 1996

Childs G., *Education and Beyond*, Floris Books, 1996

Cloos W., *The Living Earth*, Lanthorn Press, 1977

Grosse R., *The Living Being Anthroposophia*, Steiner Book Centre, 1986

Gulbekian S., *At the Grave of Civilization?* Temple Lodge Publishing, 1996

Hahn H., 'The Birth of the Waldorf School from the Threefold Social Movement' in von Poturzyn M, *Rudolf Steiner: Recollections by Some of His Pupils*, Rudolf Steiner Press, 1958

O'Connor D.J., *Free Will*, McMillan, 1972

Prokoffief S., *The Heavenly Sophia and the Being Anthroposophia*, Temple Lodge, 1996

Read H., *The Meaning of Art*, Pelican Books, 1949

Wachsmuth G., *The Evolution of Mankind*, Philosophical-Anthroposophical Press, 1961